SCHOOL
OF THE
MIRACULOUS

SCHOOL
OF THE
MIRACULOUS

A PRACTICAL GUIDE TO WALKING IN DAILY MIRACLES

KYNAN BRIDGES

WHITAKER
HOUSE

Unless otherwise indicated, all Scripture quotations are taken from the *King James Version Easy Read Bible*, KJVER®, © 2001, 2007, 2010, 2015 by Whitaker House. Used by permission. All rights reserved. Scripture quotations marked (KJV) are taken from the King James Version of the Holy Bible. Scripture quotations referenced *The Message* Bible are taken from *The Message: The Bible in Contemporary Language* by Eugene H. Peterson, © 1993, 1994, 1995, 1996, 2000, 2001, 2002. Used by permission of NavPress Publishing Group. All rights reserved. Represented by Tyndale House Publishers, Inc. Scripture quotations marked (NIV) are taken from the Holy Bible, New International Version®, NIV®, © 1973, 1978, 1984, 2011 by Biblica, Inc.® Used by permission of Zondervan. All rights reserved worldwide. www.zondervan.com. The "NIV" and "New International Version" are trademarks registered in the United States Patent and Trademark Office by Biblica, Inc.® Scripture quotations marked (NASB) are taken from the updated *New American Standard Bible*®, NASB®, © 1960, 1962, 1963, 1968, 1971, 1972, 1973, 1975, 1977, 1995 by The Lockman Foundation. Used by permission. (www.Lockman. org). Scripture quotations marked (AMP) are taken from The Amplified® Bible, © 2015 by The Lockman Foundation, La Habra, CA. Used by permission. (www.Lockman.org). All rights reserved.

Boldface type in the Scripture quotations indicates the author's emphasis. The forms LORD and GOD (in small capital letters) in Bible quotations represent the Hebrew name for God *Yahweh* (Jehovah), while *Lord* and *God* normally represent the name *Adonai*, in accordance with the Bible version used.

Some definitions of Greek words are taken from the New Testament Greek Lexicon—King James Version, based on Thayer's and Smith's Bible Dictionary, plus others (public domain), www.BibleStudyTools.com. Some definitions of Hebrew words are taken from the Old Testament Hebrew Lexicon—King James Version or New American Standard, which is the Brown, Driver, Briggs, Gesenius Lexicon (public domain), BibleStudyTools.com. Other Greek and Hebrew definitions are taken from the resources of blueletterbible.org, the electronic version of *Strong's Exhaustive Concordance of the Bible*, STRONG, (© 1980, 1986, and assigned to World Bible Publishers, Inc. Used by permission. All rights reserved.), and *Vine's Complete Expository Dictionary of Old and New Testament Words*, © 1985 by Thomas Nelson, Inc., Publishers, Nashville, TN. All rights reserved.

Unless otherwise indicated, all dictionary definitions are taken from OxfordDictionairies.com, Oxford University Press, © 2019.

SCHOOL OF THE MIRACULOUS:
A Practical Guide to Walking in Daily Miracles

Kynan Bridges Ministries, Inc.
P.O. Box 159 • Ruskin, FL 33575
www.kynanbridges.com
info@kynanbridges.com

ISBN: 978-1-64123-304-0 • eBook ISBN: 978-1-64123-305-7
Printed in the United States of America
© 2020 by Kynan Bridges

Whitaker House
1030 Hunt Valley Circle • New Kensington, PA 15068
www.whitakerhouse.com

Library of Congress Control Number: 2019952795

1 2 3 4 5 6 7 8 9 10 11 **ⱳ** 27 26 25 24 23 22 21 20

DEDICATION

I dedicate this book to the Lord Jesus Christ, the King of Kings and Lord of Lords. I also dedicate it to Gloria Bridges—my lovely, awesome, and virtuous wife, the mother of my five children, and my number-one partner and supporter in life and ministry; I love you more than words can express. Additionally, I want to dedicate this book to all those who are in need of a breakthrough—all those who are longing to experience "more" in their personal relationship with God. It is written to the millions of believers who know deep down inside that God wants them to live a supernatural life. My prayer is that you will access the heavenly realm and release supernatural and superabundant breakthrough. God bless!

CONTENTS

FOREWORD

God desires to give us destiny-changing encounters with Him, miracles, and other spiritual blessings. However, we often need to be instructed on how to receive them as we grow in our knowledge of God and His Word. When we draw closer to the Lord and put His principles for walking in the supernatural into practice, we will live in the power of the heavenly realm and receive these spiritual manifestations.

For forty years, and in over fifty nations, I have equipped and trained believers in such principles. It's been my passion to help people grow in intimacy and communion with God, receive and impart revelation, walk in effective Spirit-led ministry, and live an overcoming Christian life while extending the kingdom of God. I have devoted much of my time to teaching others according to the truths of the Scriptures, and I desire to see the body of Christ empowered by the Holy Spirit to spread the good news of Jesus Christ, as the Lord *"confirm*[s] *the word with signs following"* (Mark 16:20).

That's why I am excited about this book by Dr. Kynan Bridges, *School of the Miraculous: A Practical Guide to Walking in Daily Miracles.* Many believers feel they could never live the kind of miraculous lifestyle that other believers seem to. And most followers of Christ have yet to understand how they can walk in the miraculous *continually*—in fact, *every day*. With an excellent selection of topics and many personal illustrations, Dr. Kynan knowledgeably guides you through the process of entering into the realm of the supernatural so you can live in it daily.

God desires to meet our needs, but His plan is that we also reach out to others with His miraculous power. That is why this book contains such a vital message for both individual believers and the church as a whole. Let me share this excerpt:

> Miracles are one of the keys of the kingdom. Miracles authenticate the message of the cross, demonstrate the power of God, and draw people to the King and His kingdom. Today, the manifestation of the supernatural in the church is overdue! There is a family member who is waiting for you to embrace the full message of the kingdom and show them how real God is. There is a fellow employee waiting for you to demonstrate the power and love of Jesus in your job and in your personal life.... We are to go into all the world and make disciples, teaching them to obey what Jesus has commanded. We have been commissioned by God to teach His supernatural ways to all nations.

As we learn to walk in the realm of the miraculous, we will be able to take the power of the gospel everywhere we go and into every situation we encounter. Then, as Dr. Kynan affirms, we will be able to say with conviction—to ourselves and to those we meet—"Something good (miraculous) is going to happen to you today!"

—*James W. Goll*
President, God Encounters Ministries
Author, *The Seer, The Discerner,* and *Strike the Mark*

PREFACE

This book was born from my experiences over the years in talking with thousands of believers who were greatly discouraged and frustrated because they had heard about the power of God to meet their needs and the needs of those around them, but they weren't seeing its activity in their lives. Their inability to access God's power was leaving them without the help they desperately needed. The idea began to form in my mind of writing a handbook on walking in the miraculous—a "Miracles 101" course, a *School of the Miraculous*.

I hope you will enroll! In this book, I lay a strong biblical foundation for the present-day work and ministry of the Holy Spirit and share revelatory keys on how to live in the miraculous daily. The body of Christ lacks teaching on this vital topic, and I have designed this practical guide so that every believer can learn to operate according to God's power.

The goal of *School of the Miraculous* is to demystify the process of receiving miracles. We often have the idea that a miracle is a rare event, but this is not a biblical perspective. We can identify specific spiritual steps that will free us and enable us to live daily in the miraculous, and I am passionate about walking you through each one. We will cover such topics as

"Developing a Supernatural Culture," "Knowing Our Identity," "Breaking the Stronghold of Fear," "The Spirit of Awakening," "Everyday Miracles and the Power of Prayer," and "Five Keys to Activating God's Power." Throughout all the chapters of *School of the Miraculous*, you will discover how to experience the presence of God in your life, overcome spiritual roadblocks to victory, recognize and unlock the gifts of the Spirit, declare God's Word, and release His supernatural power.

When we develop an intimate relationship with God's Holy Spirit—the Miracle Worker—we will live in the power of the miraculous. I can confirm from my own life, and from the lives of many others, that "everyday" people can see the miraculous power of God working on their behalf. In fact, I expect to see a miracle every day! I pray that this expectation will capture your heart, as well, and that you will begin to walk in the miraculous purposes that God has planned for you.

ACKNOWLEDGMENTS

First of all, I want to take a moment and acknowledge my precious Lord Jesus Christ. It is through Him that I am able to write this and all books. To my wife—you mean more than life itself. Thank you for standing with me through the years. To my ministerial staff, thank you! To my church family (Grace & Peace Global Fellowship), who have been instrumental in praying for and supporting this project—thank you! To the team at Whitaker House—thank you for your hard work and prayerful support in helping to get this message to the world. I am grateful for all that you do. Special thanks to the production and editing team, including Christine Whitaker and Lois Puglisi at Whitaker; Crystal Dixon, Patricia Holdsworth, Camilla Hippolyte, Gloria Bridges, Ella Bridges, and the entire Kynan Bridges Ministries Team, to name a few.

I also want to take a moment to acknowledge great men and women of the faith who have impacted my life and ministry in a positive way (either directly or indirectly), including: Pastor Wayne

C. Thompson, Dr. Mark Chironna, John G. Lake, Derek Prince, Dr. Charles Stanley, Oswald Chambers, Smith Wigglesworth, John Wesley, Jack Coe, Oral Roberts, Kathryn Kuhlman, R.W. Shambach, Sid Roth, Pastor Marlin D. Harris, Mike Bickle, Hank and Brenda Kunneman, Joan Hunter, Dr. E. V. Hill, Marilyn Hickey, Pastor Tony Kemp, Dr. Douglas Wingate, Evangelist Reinhard Bonnke, Dr. Rodney Howard-Browne, Dr. T. L. Lowery, and Dr. Myles Munroe.

1

GOD'S PURPOSE FOR MIRACLES

"Verily, I say to you, he that believes on Me,
the works that I do shall he do also; and greater works
than these shall he do; because I go to My Father."
—John 14:12

I will never forget my first notable experience with the supernatural power of God. I was in a Baptist church on a Sunday evening for their "Anointing Service." Little did I know that this was not your typical Baptist church, nor was this your typical Sunday night service. I felt there was something strange and uncanny about the atmosphere, although not in an unpleasant way.

At this time in my life, I was a fairly new Christian with only a basic understanding of the gospel. It wasn't until later that I became involved in what is commonly known as the "charismatic movement."[1] I stood in that

---

1. A movement encompassing both nondenominational and denominational churches that began around the mid-twentieth century and continues today, emphasizing the baptism, gifts, and power of the Holy Spirit.

sanctuary full of skepticism and criticism as people were being ministered to by the preacher. It seemed to me as if he was pushing them down onto the floor. I thought to myself, "How could they let him make them fall like that?" I also remember thinking that this preacher would never make me fall! But before the thought could even take root in my mind, I was already on the floor! (Because of this experience, I am almost certain that God has a sense of humor.)

"What just happened to me?" I wondered. I know now that this experience is what many Christians refer to as being "slain in the Spirit," but at the time, I had no clue what it was all about. I simply knew that God's presence filled me, and I have not been the same since. I received new peace, joy, and confidence. If you are not familiar with this experience, it probably sounds as strange to you as it did to me at first. But this phenomenon occurs when the presence or anointing of God is so strong that it literally causes people to drop to the floor—without any injury—and sometimes to appear unconscious. During this time, the Lord ministers to their spirit and emotions, manifesting His presence and bringing healing. It is a way of drawing them to Himself—spirit, soul, and body—for a special time of surrender and ministry.

Though I would not consider my experience that day to be a miracle according to the biblical definition, it was the beginning of many supernatural encounters with God and His miraculous power that have profoundly transformed my life. Millions of believers have had the same experience.

THE POWER OF GOD TODAY

On the other hand, a number of Christians wonder if miracles were only relevant during the first century when the church was being established by the first apostles. They don't see how they could possibly be available for us today. Other Christians know about the power of God and are eager to have it manifest in their lives, but are greatly disappointed and frustrated because they have never experienced it firsthand or have seen it only rarely.

Can every believer operate in the power and gifts of the Holy Spirit? I want to assure you that everyday Christians around the world are seeing the miraculous power of God move in their lives—and the same can be true for you. It is happening because these believers have come into an awareness of the spiritual realm, and they have a lifestyle of walking in the Spirit, which gives them access to heaven's resources. We cannot access something if we are not aware of it! *But revelation releases miracles.* A renewed understanding of God's purposes will open the door to the miraculous in your life.

GOD'S ETERNAL PURPOSES FOR MIRACLES

Throughout Scripture, it is clear that miracles are part of God's plan for interrupting the natural course of human operations. In other words, He always manifests His supernatural power to show us that His agenda is infinitely more significant than our agenda (unless our agenda is already His agenda!). Miracles are powerful because they reveal something higher and greater than ourselves and this physical world.

There is more to Christianity than singing songs and attending church services. The God of the Bible is very real. He is alive and well! Through the power of miracles, He invades time with His eternal purposes. Miracles, signs, and wonders are God's signposts in the earthly realm. They point to the eternal King and His kingdom of *"righteousness, and peace, and joy in the Holy Ghost"* (Romans 14:17).

We could say that signs and wonders are the spiritual advertisements of the power of God's kingdom. Just as a street sign tells you what lies ahead, God's signs and wonders point the unbeliever and believer alike to the power of the world to come. Jesus told us:

And these signs shall follow them that believe; In my name shall they cast out devils; they shall speak with new tongues; they shall take up serpents; and if they drink any deadly thing, it shall not hurt them; they shall lay hands on the sick, and they shall recover.

—Mark 16:17–18

The word *"signs"* in this verse is translated from the Greek word *sēmeion*, which means "a sign, mark, token." It can refer to "an unusual occurrence,

SECRET TO THE SUPERNATURAL:

CREATE AN ATMOSPHERE OF WORSHIP AND ADORATION

WHERE JESUS IS EXALTED AND

THE PRESENCE OF GOD IS MANIFESTED.

MIRACLES COME EASILY IN SUCH AN ATMOSPHERE.

transcending the common course of nature: of miracles and wonders by which God authenticates the men sent by him, or by which men prove that the cause they are pleading is God's." The Greek word rendered "*follow*" is *parakoloutheō*, which means "to follow after"; "so to follow one as to be always at his side"; "to follow close, accompany." Note that the Scriptures say these signs "*follow*" or "accompany" the believer. We are never to chase signs and wonders for their own sake. Instead, they should accompany us as we proclaim and pursue the kingdom of God.

THE POWER OF FOLLOWING GOD'S "SYSTEMS"

God is a God of patterns and systems. A *pattern* can be defined as "a regular and intelligible form or sequence discernible in certain actions or situations." Just as there are natural systems, or established ways of doing things, which we can follow and see clearly defined and measurable outcomes, there are spiritual systems in the kingdom of God. Contrary to what some people think, there is nothing random about God. Everything He does is intentional. Many believers want to see miracles, but they fail to understand that miracles are conditional on implementing and responding to various divine systems.

For example, Matthew 6:33 says, *"But seek you first the kingdom of God, and His righteousness; and all these things shall be added to you."* The Bible clearly instructs us to seek first God's kingdom and righteousness in our lives. The kingdom of God is His government and dominion over every sphere of reality. As we proclaim the kingdom, we activate the inevitable result: miracles. When Jesus preached the kingdom, healings occurred, demons were evicted, people were set free from oppression, and miracles happened!

CREATIVE MIRACLES

I vividly remember a time when I was preaching in Australia, and there was a man present who'd permanently injured one of his eyes in a motorcycle accident. The connective tissue between his eyeball and his brain had been disconnected, resulting in total blindness in that eye. He had been in that condition for over six years, yet as I preached the Word of God, this gentleman felt a "pop" in his eye, and all of a sudden, he could see. He was in utter shock! He began to weep as he beckoned to his wife to inform her of what had happened. They were so excited and filled with joy.

No one had placed their hands on him and prayed for him. But the message of the kingdom releases miracles. Because the spiritual atmosphere had been established and Jesus had been glorified in the meeting, the presence and power of God were manifested and healing came.

THESE SIGNS SHALL FOLLOW US

"And these signs shall follow them that believe…." We must remember that signs and wonders are destined to *follow* believers, not the other way around. As we seek the kingdom of God, according to Matthew 6:33, and proclaim the gospel, certain results must take place:

1. Satan's kingdom of darkness will be cast out and demonic powers will be subdued.

2. Believers will be given the ability to speak with new languages, either heavenly or earthly tongues (I will talk more about this gift later on).

3. Believers will experience divine protection.

4. The sick will be healed supernaturally.

While I do not believe these are the only signs that are to follow believers in Jesus, they are a starting point for every disciple of Christ. Jesus said, *"He that believes on Me, the works that I do shall he do also; and greater works than these shall he do; because I go to My Father."*

Every believer in Jesus can operate in the miraculous power of God daily. In fact, it is a promise from God that we will see such spiritual manifestations regularly if we follow the New Testament pattern. Unfortunately, too many Christians have believed a false gospel, what I call the "gospel of exclusion." This is the belief that the message of the cross—forgiveness for sin—is enough. Because the gospel of exclusion essentially ignores the glorious implications of Christ's resurrection, it is a powerless message in terms of living the kingdom lifestyle.

It is not enough for us to attend Sunday services and midweek Bible studies. Of course, learning about faith in Jesus is essential. However, there must also be a tangible expression of God's power in our lives because this, too, is an important aspect of having faith in Jesus. Such expressions should be present in our lives every day! I submit to you that a Christianity void of the demonstration of God's kingdom and power is not New Testament Christianity at all.

Now, I know that is a very strong statement. I made it intentionally. Why? Because there are scores of Christians who have yet to experience the God of the Bible. Again, the God we serve is alive and well. He desires to demonstrate His power in our lives in a tangible way. "For the eyes of the LORD run to and fro throughout the whole earth, to show Himself strong in the behalf of them whose heart is perfect toward Him" (2 Chronicles 16:9).

THE "PACKAGE" YOU RECEIVED

One of the Greek words translated "miracles" in the New Testament is *dunamis*, among whose meanings is "power for performing miracles." This is the term from which we derive the English word *dynamite*. The word picture here is very vivid. God's power is like dynamite! This is the word the apostle Paul used in Romans 1:16:

*I am not ashamed of the gospel of Christ: for it is the **power** of God to salvation to every one that believes; to the Jew first, and also to the Greek.*

Paul equated the gospel of Jesus Christ with the power to perform miracles, or miracle-working power. This fact should make us ask, "How can we call what we preach or proclaim 'the gospel' if there is no *dunamis*, or demonstrative supernatural power?" When Jesus preached, there was demonstration. When the apostles preached, there was demonstration. When we preach, there should be demonstration! You don't need a special religious degree or spiritual certificate to walk in the supernatural. It is included in the "package" you were given when you received Christ as your Savior and Lord. Jesus told His disciples,

---

But you shall receive power, after that the Holy Ghost is come upon you: and you shall be witnesses to Me both in Jerusalem, and in all Judaea, and in Samaria, and to the uttermost part of the earth.

—Acts 1:8

The Greek word for *"power"* here is the same word that we have been discussing: *dunamis.* The Holy Spirit provides every believer with miracle power. The question is, what are we going to do with it? Power that is not recognized is power that is not released, and power that is not released is power that is not realized.

This is why the baptism in the Holy Spirit is a key element in experiencing the miraculous power of God. Being baptized in the Spirit of God is a necessary element of victorious Christian living. The Bible actually commands us, *"Be filled with the Spirit"* (Ephesians 5:18). We are to be immersed in the presence and power of God's Spirit. John the Baptist said, *"I indeed baptize you with water to repentance: but He that comes after me is mightier than I, whose shoes I am not worthy to bear: He shall baptize you with the Holy Ghost, and with fire"* (Matthew 3:11). Jesus came to baptize us with the Holy Spirit and fire. This is a promise from God. Yet there are many people who have yet to receive this baptism, which is distinct from the salvation experience, although it is possible for them to take place simultaneously.

Just like any gift in the kingdom of God, we must receive the baptism by faith. Jesus said, *"If you then, being evil, know how to give good gifts to your children: how much more shall your heavenly Father give the Holy Spirit to them that ask Him?"* (Luke 11:13). All you have to do is ask! Would you like to receive the baptism in the Holy Spirit right now? If so, please pray this prayer with me:

Father, I thank You that You are the giver of good gifts. You promised in Your Word that You would give the gift of the Holy Spirit to those who ask. Therefore, I ask You for the baptism in the Holy Spirit, accompanied by the gift of speaking in tongues as the Spirit gives utterance. Thank You for Your presence and power filling me right now. In Jesus's name, amen!

A POWERFUL ENGINE

For various reasons, many Christians have not yet recognized the full potential of a Spirit-filled life. They are like an automobile with a powerful engine that has never been driven more than twenty miles an hour. Some have never even left the parking lot! Jesus paid the ultimate price to release His power in and through us, but we must put the key in the ignition and "put the pedal to the medal." In other words, we need to "put a claim," or "place a demand," on God's miraculous power.

If you want to see a miracle in your life, especially a miracle operating through you, you must place a claim on heaven! In my experience with God, I have found that the greater the risk, the greater the reward. In the kingdom of God, faith is spelled R-I-S-K:

1. *Release* your faith for more.

2. *Instigate* heaven by stepping out.

3. *Stand* on the Word of God.

4. *Keep* pressing until you see a miracle.

The more we step out and take a risk (such as praying for someone or proclaiming the gospel), the more heaven will meet us at the point of faith and expectancy.

PRAYER FOR MIRACLE POWER

Father, in the name of Your Son Jesus Christ, I thank You for Your presence and power in my life. I know that miracles are from You,

SECRET TO THE SUPERNATURAL:

THE GREATER THE DEMAND PLACED,

THE GREATER THE MANIFESTATION RECEIVED.

and I desire to live a supernatural life. By faith, I receive and release Your *dunamis* power, the power to perform miracles! I recognize that the Holy Spirit is the source of supernatural power for the believer; therefore, I receive anew the infilling of the Holy Spirit. As I yield to Your Spirit, Your miracle power flows through every fiber of my being. I will never be the same again! In Jesus's name, amen!

MIRACLE INSIGHTS

1. Why don't some Christians believe in miracles today? What is this viewpoint called?

2. What does the Greek word *dunamis* have to do with the miraculous? What is the Bible referring to when it mentions *dunamis* power?

3. What is the correlation between the Holy Spirit and miracles?

4. What does it mean to take a R-I-S-K in the kingdom of God?

MIRACLE TESTIMONY

A MIRACULOUS HEALING

A young girl in our church heard our teaching on miracles, signs, and wonders, and began to put it into practice. Even though she did not come from a Christian background, God began to do a work in her as she learned to yield to the Holy Spirit. One day, she was talking with her grandmother, who had been dealing with a chronic health condition for many years, and she began to release her faith for miracles, declaring her grandmother's healing in Jesus's name. Her grandmother was miraculously healed. This healing did not come through a televangelist or prominent Christian minister, but through a ten-year-old child! Every believer can operate in the miraculous power of God.

2

HEAVEN INVADING EARTH

"Your kingdom come. Your will be done in earth,
as it is in heaven."
—Matthew 6:10

An understanding of the kingdom of God is central to our Christian walk, yet many people in the Western world, including Christians, don't really understand the concept of a kingdom. This is especially true in societies that base their government on the concept of democracy. For instance, the United States is a representative democracy, governed "by the people, for the people." Though this is a great form of government, it does not operate in the same way the kingdom of God is governed.

WHAT IS A KINGDOM?

The word *kingdom* literally means "the domain of the king." It is an expression of government, power, rule, and authority in a particular territory. A kingdom typically expands in two ways: conquest or colonization.

When a kingdom conquers another kingdom or territory, it establishes its rulership and dominion over that territory.

Colonization is defined as "the action or process of settling among and establishing control over the indigenous people of an area." I know that the concept of colonization has a very negative connotation in our culture, but this is indeed the way a kingdom establishes control over foreign populations. It involves the appropriation of culture, language, and customs.

WHAT IS THE KINGDOM OF GOD?

For the kingdom of God is not meat and drink; but righteousness, and peace, and joy in the Holy Ghost.   —Romans 14:17

The kingdom of God is His kingship, authority, influence, and government in the entire universe, especially in the earth. While the kingdom of heaven is a place, not merely a geographical place as we know them, the kingdom of God is a system. This system is characterized by righteousness, peace, and joy in the Holy Spirit.

1. *Righteousness*: God's right way of doing things. Justice, judgment, and morality.

2. *Peace*: *shalom*, or completeness. Nothing missing and nothing broken.

3. *Joy*: a state of being that is void of fear, worry, anxiety, or shame.

An essential distinction between the kingdom of God and earthly kingdoms is that the territory of God's kingdom on earth was usurped by the enemy, Satan, whose sole intent is *"to steal, and to kill, and to destroy"* (John 10:10) this world, including human beings. God's kingdom continually moves to regain this lost territory and restore a rule of love, peace, and joy on the earth.

WHERE IS THE KINGDOM OF GOD?

Thus, the purpose of heaven is to colonize the earth. Jesus instructed us to pray, *"Your kingdom come. Your will be done in earth, **as it is in heaven.**"* We are ambassadors of the eternal King, empowered with the spiritual authority to release heaven into the earth—beginning with us! Notice that the King James Bible uses the expression *"in earth,"* rather than "on earth." Why is that word significant? The apostle Paul wrote, *"But we have this treasure in earthen vessels, that the excellency of the power may be of God, and not of us"* (2 Corinthians 4:7). We are the earthen vessels. God wants His kingdom to be established within us.

Until heaven manifests in us, it cannot manifest on earth. As we yield to the kingdom *in* us, we begin to see the manifestation of the kingdom *through* us. We experience the demonstration of the kingdom by yielding to the government of God in our lives. As a result, the Holy Spirit colonizes the earth around us through His presence and power. This is the real purpose of miracles. The power of God is not meant to impress us or gratify our religious sentiments but to show the world that God is indeed King and His kingdom reigns over all the earth.

Miracles, signs, and wonders are the evidentiary proof that heaven can and must invade our world. God is demonstrating His sovereignty over every other human or satanic kingdom in existence. Jesus said, *"But if I with the finger of God cast out devils, no doubt the kingdom of God is come upon you"* (Luke 11:20). Every time He cast out demons, it was confirmation that the kingdom had come.

I will never forget an incident that occurred when I was preaching to a large crowd overseas. A young man yelled out, "What is he talking about?" in a very disrespectful and disruptive manner. At first, I chose to ignore it. Then, he yelled again, "What is he talking about?" At that point, I called out, "You foul devil! Don't say another word, in the name of Jesus!" The entire congregation appeared shocked, and a blanket of silence came over the auditorium. I hadn't been speaking to the young man himself but rather to the demonic spirit that was operating through him. Then, I simply continued preaching as if nothing had happened. The young man never said another word.

After the service, the local pastor approached me concerning my strong statement, informing me that this man had Asperger syndrome and was often disruptive. He further told me that he had apologized to the mother on my behalf, just in case she had been offended. However, the mother had replied that she hadn't been offended at all. In fact, she had said, "Please thank the pastor, because my son has not been that peaceful in eight years!" Praise God! (I believe that many people who have been diagnosed with a medical condition are experiencing demonic oppression. However, not every illness or condition is related to demonic attack.)

The kingdom of God came to that mother and her son, demonstrating once again that the light of God is greater than the darkness in the world, and that the kingdom of God is superior to the kingdom of this world.

COMMISSIONED TO RELEASE GOD'S KINGDOM

The truth is that every single believer has been called and commissioned to release God's kingdom wherever they go. I want you to begin thinking of miracles as one of heaven's main ways of invading the earth for kingdom purposes, rather than as random occurrences that happen every now and then when God decides to give them.

I am reminded of a lovely couple who came to our ministry. The husband was unemployed and the wife was experiencing tremendous spiritual warfare, including health challenges. They were literally on the brink of divorce. The husband started to withdraw from the church community, but the wife continued to press in to God's Word. She kept coming to church and giving. Then the Lord began to speak to them both. As we continued to pray, God began to deliver the wife, and the couple's faith and marriage were restored. Their finances were also restored supernaturally. God is a God of miracles! If you will dare to contend for the supernatural, heaven will invade the earth.

When Jesus walked the earth, He released miracles everywhere He went. As a result of His ministry, the sick were healed, lepers were cleansed, the blind received sight, the deaf were enabled to hear, and people experienced a tangible touch from God. The same ministry can happen through you and me. As ambassadors of God's kingdom, we have been charged with the responsibility of advancing the kingdom on earth, in all spheres of influence.

How can we do this? The first requirement is availability. We must make ourselves available to God in obedient submission to His Word. Unless we obey the Word of God, our quest for the miraculous will be fruitless. I challenge you to say, "Lord, I am available to You!"

Our willingness to yield to God is a major factor in seeing the manifestation of His power through us. I cannot overstate the importance of this condition. God rewards our willingness!

If you be willing and obedient, you shall eat the good of the land.
— Isaiah 1:19

What does the Bible mean by willingness? Willingness refers to our ability and desire to cooperate with God and His Word. There are many people, including Christians, who do not live a life of obedience to God's Word. Some of them actually operate in rebellion. If you live in disobedience, God will not consistently manifest His power through you.

Surrender is more than an intellectual concept; it is a spiritual posture. When we surrender to God, we are telling Him that He has the right to direct our lives. We submit to His lordship, and then we become recipients of His delivering power.

Some people want to know Jesus as Savior, but they don't want to submit to Him as Lord. The word *Lord* comes from the Greek word *kurios*, which can refer to a landlord or property owner. Let me be clear: God does not exist for our pleasure; we exist for His. This is a very important truth that must be understood. Jesus is our Landlord, Owner, and Administrator. Our lives belong to Him! His will for our lives must prevail. If you want

SECRET TO THE SUPERNATURAL:

IN THE KINGDOM OF GOD, TRUE POWER COMES FROM SURRENDER. THE MORE SURRENDERED YOU ARE, THE MORE GOD'S POWER CAN FLOW THROUGH YOU!

to advance the kingdom of God, you must submit to the lordship of Jesus Christ daily. Remember, He is the sovereign King. When you submit to the agenda of the King, you will always see the manifestation of His kingdom. I invite you to pray this prayer of surrender today.

PRAYER OF SURRENDER

Father, I thank You for Your kingdom and majesty! As I yield to you in total surrender, I ask you to manifest your kingdom in and through me. Forgive me for the areas in my life that I have not submitted to you. Forgive for me for exercising self-will. I fully confess my sin of disobedience and receive the truth of Your Word. I thank You that I am Your ambassador on earth, and that Your agenda is my agenda! I declare that when people see me, they will see Jesus and the culture of the kingdom of God. I embrace my ambassadorial assignment to advance Your kingdom on earth, within my circle of influence. I advance Your kingdom by operating in signs, wonders, and miracles. Thank You for all Your goodness! In Jesus's name, amen!

MIRACLE INSIGHTS

1. What does the Bible mean by the term "kingdom of God"?

2. When we receive God's Spirit, where is the kingdom of God located?

3. How do we release the kingdom of God in a practical way? What biblical examples do we have of releasing the kingdom?

4. What part does surrender play in our walking in miracles?

SCHOOL OF THE MIRACULOUS PRACTICUM

1. Read and meditate on Matthew 6:10 and 2 Corinthians 4:7, and then think about how God wants to establish His kingdom in you. Write down ways in which you may be trying to rely on your own abilities instead of God's strength to bring His kingdom to earth, and release those areas to Him.

2. Begin to pray daily that God will show you specific ways in which He wants to use you to spread His kingdom on earth. Each day, pray, "Lord, I am available to You!"

3. Has God been directing you to reach out to someone in your sphere of influence? Step out in faith this week to contact that person, asking the Lord to use you to demonstrate His love and the power of His kingdom.

3

DEVELOPING A SUPERNATURAL CULTURE

"For our conversation [manner of lifestyle, culture, citizenship]
is in heaven; from where also we look for the Savior,
the Lord Jesus Christ."
—Philippians 3:20

I remember the first time I traveled to a country outside of the United States. Because the environment was so different from what I was used to, I had to make some major adjustments in my perspective! Some of what I encountered was astonishing to me. This kind of experience is often referred to as "culture shock." However, the more I engaged the people in that country, the more I began to understand and embrace their culture. Since that time, I've followed a similar process as I've traveled extensively throughout the world. I have now been to most of the continents and have learned the significance of culture.

Culture is defined as "the customs, arts, social institutions, and achievements of a particular nation, people, or other social group." So, when I talk

SECRET TO THE SUPERNATURAL:

ABSORBING THE CULTURE OF THE SUPERNATURAL IS A

KEY TO RELEASING GOD'S POWER.

about culture, I am referring to the pervasive mind-sets, attitudes, worldviews, and behaviors that govern a group of people. The concept of "group" includes families, tribes, and nations.

The Bible says that our *"conversation* [manner of lifestyle, culture, citizenship] *is in heaven."* What does this mean? It means that, as believers, you and I have become citizens of a heavenly kingdom that has a distinct culture, and we must become infused with that culture if we want to live the Christian life successfully. An integral feature of this culture is supernatural power.

In the natural world, everything we see and experience is affected by and processed through the lens of our particular culture. As we grow in our understanding of the culture of God's kingdom (and spiritual matters in general), we will gain a God-centered outlook on the world. To walk in the supernatural, we must learn the culture of the kingdom and live in harmony with it.

PRIMARY COMPONENTS OF KINGDOM CULTURE

There are two main components to any culture: language and customs. Let's look at the characteristics of each in relation to God's kingdom.

THE LANGUAGE OF THE SUPERNATURAL

My pastor always emphasized that there are basically two things that separate people from one another: culture and language (which we are including here as an element of culture). This statement is very true! If we are going to develop a supernatural lifestyle, we must begin by understanding the language of the supernatural.

Language can be defined as "a system of communication used by a particular country or community." When we were born again, we became a part of the beloved community called the church, which exists within the greater realm of God's kingdom. (See, for example, Matthew 16:18; Acts 2.) Like any kingdom, the kingdom of God has a distinct language. In my view, the primary language of the kingdom and its supernatural culture is *faith.*

SECRET TO THE SUPERNATURAL:

PRACTICE SPEAKING THE WORD OF GOD DAILY, INCLUDING RECITING PARTICULAR SCRIPTURES AND READING THE BIBLE ALOUD. BE WILLING TO CONFORM YOUR THINKING TO THE WORD OF GOD CONSISTENTLY.

And Jesus answering said to them, Have faith in God. For verily I say to you, That whosoever shall say to this mountain, Be you removed, and be you cast into the sea; and shall not doubt in his heart, but shall believe that those things which he says shall come to pass; he shall have whatsoever he says. Therefore I say to you, What things soever you desire, when you pray, believe that you receive them, and you shall have them.

—Mark 11:22–24

Notice that this Scripture is very specific. We are to have faith in God, and then *say* to the mountain…. If you want to see the miraculous, you need to declare God's living words every day in faith. You must learn to open your mouth and speak faith-filled words. Many people underestimate the power of speaking the Word daily, but it has the potential to radically transform your life, to the glory of God. (We will talk further about this practice in chapter 7, "The Authority of Proclamation.")

Faith is the language of the supernatural!

COMMUNICATING WITH GOD

Imagine two people who speak totally different languages trying to talk to one another. It would prove to be a very frustrating experience. Neither could understand what the other was saying. Many believers experience a similar frustration. They are making requests of God for healings, miracles, restoration, and breakthrough, but they don't speak the language that heaven "understands." God communicates through the language of faith. "But **without faith it** *is impossible to please Him: for he that comes to God must believe that He is, and that He is a rewarder of them that diligently seek Him*" (Hebrews 11:6).

Instead of speaking the language of faith, many people speak the language of doubt and unbelief. Doubt and unbelief are a foreign language in God's kingdom. As we know, the purpose of language is communication. It is through faith that we communicate to God what we request of Him, with the expectation that He will answer us. God responds to expectation. When we doubt Him, we are telling Him that He is not as powerful as He claims to be. Whoa! You probably never thought about it that way, but that is exactly the way it is!

Just like any language, faith has a syntax. *Syntax* refers to "the arrangement of words and phrases to create well-formed sentences in a language," or "a set of rules for or an analysis of the syntax of a language." People often say that prayer and receiving from God are not about formulas, and I certainly agree. However, there is a clear distinction between faith-filled words and doubt-filled words and the outcomes they produce. It is almost shocking to listen to what some Christians say. The level of cynicism, negativity, and doubt that I often hear coming from the mouths of Christians is astounding to me. Whenever they do that, they release negativity into their lives. But when we express faith, we are communicating and activating the syntax of heaven. Faith is essential to releasing God's supernatural power in your life.

We might say that the spiritual realm is "voice-activated." The nature of your words determines the nature of your world. Faith speaks! Second Corinthians 4:13 says, *"Having the same spirit of faith, according as it is written, I believed, and therefore have I spoken; we also believe, and therefore speak."* Again, notice that the Scripture says we believe, and therefore we speak. Faith always speaks according to the Word of God. In this way, faith accesses supernatural doors. Just as a key card communicates a digital code that opens a specific door, faith communicates the "code" of the supernatural that grants access to miracles, signs, and wonders. The question is, do we really believe God?

Faith is the substance of things hoped for, the evidence of things not seen. —Hebrews 11:1

Please understand that faith doesn't *make* God do anything, but it does grant us access to what He has already done. Faith is the currency of the kingdom of God. It is the medium of exchange that allows you to make transactions in the kingdom. We often hear the expression "Money talks," and in the natural world, that is often the case! In other words, money is the language that many people understand and respond to. In a similar way, faith "talks." It is both the language and the currency that heaven responds to.

RECEIVING BY FAITH

The greater your faith, the greater your access to the supernatural. Understanding this truth transformed my life and ministry. Everything that my wife and I have received from God, we have received by faith, and the ministry of the miraculous is no exception.

When we know the Word, faith comes into manifestation and situations begin to change. Imagine for a moment that someone had a serious illness and came to you for prayer. You have two choices: You can stay trapped in a bubble of insecurity and fear, wondering, "What if nothing happens?" or "What if my prayer isn't answered?" Or, you can release your faith and see the manifestation of God's power. A prayer never prayed can never be answered, and a demand never placed can never be met!

One day, I was praying for a woman who had not walked without a walker for nine years. Her veins were damaged and she had been suffering the effects of diabetes. Yet, in one of our meetings, she decided to take a "leap of faith." She made her way to the front of the church with the assistance of her daughter, and I prayed a quick prayer over her: "Be healed, in Jesus's name!" Nothing happened! But a short while later, we heard a scream from the back of the church. Lo and behold, this woman was dancing without any assistance. The next day, we received word that she was able to walk on her own. According to her faith, she was healed. Healing is especially effective when there is the mutual faith of the one being prayed for and the one praying.

THE CUSTOMS OF THE SUPERNATURAL

A second main component of the culture of God's kingdom is its customs. A *custom* is defined as "a traditional and widely accepted way of behaving or doing something that is specific to a particular society, place, or time." What do customs have to do with miracles? I'm glad you asked!

A LIFESTYLE OF HOLINESS

One of the primary customs of the kingdom of God is a lifestyle of holiness. Holiness is another major key to manifesting God's supernatural power in your life.

Follow peace with all men, and holiness, without which no man shall see the Lord.   —Hebrews 12:14

Without holiness, no one will see the Lord. The Greek word translated "*holiness*" is *hagiasmos*, which means "consecration, purification," and "the effect of consecration: sanctification of heart and life." Simply put, to be holy is to be set apart from all that is unclean or vile. The Bible clearly says,

---

But as He which has called you is holy, so be you holy in all manner of conversation; because it is written, Be you holy; for I am holy.
                                                    — 1 Peter 1:15–16

First, it is important to understand that holiness is not something we conjure up in our own strength. We are made holy through the blood of Jesus alone. (See, for example 1 John 1:7.) His holiness and righteousness are imputed to us by faith. (See, for example, Romans 3:22.) Though we receive holiness as a gift, we have a responsibility to walk in holiness in our daily lives. We do this by continually yielding to the leading and nature of the Holy Spirit. Remember, He is the *Holy* Spirit! This means that every "legal" manifestation of the Spirit of God must be accompanied by holiness.

If you want to walk in power, you need to live a sanctified life. You must make a deliberate and intentional decision to abstain from wrongdoing and the appearance of evil. (See, for example, 1 John 3:9; 1 Thessalonians 5:22.) You make a choice to deny your fleshly desires. (See, for example, Ephesians 4:21–23.) You become mindful of your thoughts, attitudes, and conversations, as well as what you allow into your ear and eye gates. As antiquated as this idea may seem, nothing boosts your confidence in God's ability to demonstrate His power like holiness. The older saints used to say, "Holiness is still right!"

Have you ever tried to pray for someone after you've engaged in willful sin? How do you feel afterward? Sin destroys our confidence in God. In Hebrews 12:14, we read that without holiness, no one will *see* God. This doesn't just refer to the hereafter. It means that without holiness, you cannot see the manifestation of God in your life. I don't know about you, but I want to see God and His works!

Unfortunately, we live in a culture where the idea of holiness is looked down upon, even in much of the church. Many people have mistaken the teaching of grace as a license to sin rather than understanding that grace is a supernatural empowerment to enable us to live righteously. As the church has lowered its standards, we have seen fewer and fewer demonstrations of God's power. It is time for the body of Christ to come back to the foundation, customs, and conduct of the kingdom of God, including holiness and righteousness.

The word *saints* means "sanctified" or "consecrated." Without sanctification, the saints become "aints" (an urban expression for being without something)—lacking miraculous manifestations. They cannot walk in the level of supernatural power and influence that the Father has provided for them. The devil is not intimidated by a church that looks and behaves like the world.

We must be consecrated. We must be set apart, different from the world! We must be intentional about separating ourselves from anything or anyone that would sap our spiritual power and influence. Our value as believers is in our difference, not in our conformity.

SECRET TO THE SUPERNATURAL:

THE MORE CONSECRATED YOU ARE, THE MORE SPIRITUAL

POWER AND AUTHORITY YOU WALK IN.

I beseech you therefore, brethren, by the mercies of God, that you present your bodies a living sacrifice, holy, acceptable to God, which is your reasonable service. And be not conformed to this world: but be you transformed by the renewing of your mind, that you may prove what is that good, and acceptable, and perfect, will of God.

—Romans 12:1–2

In this passage, we are admonished not to conform to this world, but to be transformed by the renewing of our mind. We must think differently if we want to see different results. The apostle Paul writes that we should *"prove,"* or demonstrate, the good, acceptable, and perfect will of God. We can only accomplish this when we think and live in a new way.

Financial expert Dave Ramsey often says, "If you want to live like no one else, you have to live like no one else." Though this statement specifically refers to finances, I believe it stands true in spiritual matters as well. If we are going to see the supernatural, we must be committed to living supernaturally.

THE PRACTICE OF SHOWING HONOR

Another vital aspect of the customs of God's kingdom is the practice of showing honor. Like faith, honor is a currency of the kingdom. To honor is to highly esteem or attach value to someone or something. One Hebrew word for honor is *kabod*, which means "weight" or "glory." God will never manifest His glory in an atmosphere of dishonor. You will notice that churches and individuals who carry the manifest presence of God embrace the kingdom culture of honor.

I had a memorable experience in this regard while preaching at a church on the West Coast. The pastors there showed me great honor. They went out of their way to make my stay welcoming and comfortable. In fact, they catered to my every need consistently! And something very interesting happened. In their services, the glory of God would literally manifest *every*

SECRET TO THE SUPERNATURAL:

THE MANIFESTATION YOU FAIL TO HONOR IS THE

MANIFESTATION YOU FAIL TO ATTRACT. WHATEVER YOU

HONOR, YOU INCREASE.

time. In one instance, I hugged the pastor during the greeting time, and God's power came, and the pastor fell to the floor under the glory of God. I asked God why this was the case. He answered me in one word: *honor.*

Honor is a catalyst for the manifestation of God's presence. Where there is no honor, there is no glory! Let me repeat that: where there is no honor, there is no glory!

Faith and honor, combined with expectancy, create the environment for miracles. You always value what you honor. What you honor, you appreciate; and what you appreciate, you accentuate. The moment something becomes common to us, it loses its impact.

Brothers and sisters, never allow your spiritual leader to become common to you. The moment that happens, the flow of grace upon that leader's life is blocked from coming into your life. Jesus Himself could not do any miracles in an atmosphere of overfamiliarity. (See Mark 13:54–58.) The anointing you respect is the anointing you release!

Remember that honor is more than an exterior expression of appreciation. It is recognizing someone's value in your heart. When we honor someone, we esteem them highly. As a result of this esteem, the tangible glory of God is released into our lives. One day, an individual reached out to our ministry, saying that they had just given a seed of honor as an expression of appreciation for the work the ministry was doing. The seed they sowed was $300. The very next day, they received $30,000. Hallelujah! Many miracles are initiated by an act of honor! We have seen hundreds of testimonies just like that one all over the world.

Some time ago, I went through one of the most difficult seasons of my life and ministry. During this time, I was preaching all over the world. As I traveled and preached, the Lord gave me very specific instructions: He told me to sow a significant financial seed into a ministry for which I was preaching at the time. Immediately, I obeyed the prompting of the Lord. As I sowed the seed, I asked that my financial seed would be considered a battle seed in the courts of heaven and that it would silence the voice of the accuser, Satan, and cause all losses to stop. After I sowed this seed, I felt something lift.

SECRET TO THE SUPERNATURAL:

FAITH ACTION IN THE NATURAL REALM PRODUCES A

RESPONSE IN THE SPIRITUAL REALM. IF YOU WANT TO

SEE HEAVEN MOVE, TAKE A STEP OF FAITH.

When I returned from overseas, the Holy Spirit spoke very clearly to my wife and me that we should host an all-night prayer meeting. So, we did just that! A number of people participated in this service, including over four thousand virtual viewers. It was extremely powerful! During the all-night prayer meeting, we prayed about very specific issues that were arising in our church. One of the issues was the need for a church building. We had been searching for an appropriate building in the area for at least five years. The very next day, we received word that a building had become available in our area. I met with the owner of the building the following day and made our interest known. Within a few days, we received the keys to the building. Hallelujah!

PRAYER FOR THE MANIFESTATION OF KINGDOM CULTURE

Father, in the name of Jesus, I thank You for who You are and all that You have done in my life. I know that You are the righteous King and Your Kingdom is always advancing in the earth. Thank You for making me one of Your citizens through the blood of Jesus Christ and the power of Your Holy Spirit. I recognize that the language of heaven is faith and the customs of heaven are holiness and honor. Thank You for the revelation of biblical honor. As I release my faith in Your Word and walk in a culture of honor, I thank You that miracles will become more common in my life. I position myself right now to see the manifestation of Your supernatural power. In the precious name of Your Son, Jesus, I pray. Amen!

MIRACLE INSIGHTS

1. How would you define culture? What does it mean to develop a supernatural culture?

2. What are the two major components to every culture? How important are language and culture in developing a supernatural lifestyle?

3. What is the "language of heaven"?

4. What is the relationship between honor and the miraculous?

MIRACLE TESTIMONY

A MIRACLE OF SALVATION

One year, my wife and I hosted a birthday party for my daughter at our house. All of her friends and their parents were invited to come. One particularly close friend came to the party with her mother. As we began conversing with this parent, we discovered some very interesting things. She was an adherent of Rastafarianism, didn't believe in the God of the Bible, and was very cynical about Christianity and organized religion in general. She had been estranged from her husband and was dealing with substance abuse. I would love to say that we had a great conversation about the Lord that led to her salvation that night, but that's the exact opposite of what happened. We argued in my living room until the next morning. But before she left, I made a prophetic declaration over her life. I said that the God of the Bible would reveal Himself to her. Several months went by. Then, my wife received a phone call from her, inquiring about our church and the specific times of the services. To our surprise, this woman came to church the next Sunday with her children. She enjoyed the service, although she was not happy about my wife attempting to lead her children to Jesus.

But she came back again! And again! Eventually, she came to the altar for salvation. A few weeks later, her estranged husband moved back in with her and came to church and prayed the prayer of salvation. Her children were born again and filled with the Spirit of God. Both she and her husband were baptized. Their finances were turned around supernaturally, and they moved into a new home. Hallelujah! Make no mistake, the greatest miracle is the miracle of salvation.

4

KNOWING OUR IDENTITY

"When Jesus came into the coasts of Caesarea Philippi,
He asked His disciples, saying,
Whom do men say that I the Son of man am?"
—Matthew 16:13

One thing is certain: if we are going to walk consistently in the miraculous power of God, we must know who we are. Understanding our identity is one of the most important aspects of our spiritual life.

Jesus asked His disciples this weighty question: *"Whom do men say that I the Son of man am?"* After they had given a laundry list of answers, including John the Baptist, Elijah, Jeremiah, or one of the other Old Testament prophets, Peter rose up and said, *"You are the Christ, the Son of the living God"* (Matthew 16:16).

Jesus told Peter that flesh and blood had not revealed this truth to him. God the Father Himself had disclosed it. Then Jesus said, *"You are Peter*

SECRET TO THE SUPERNATURAL:

IN ORDER TO KNOW WHO WE ARE,

WE MUST FIRST KNOW WHO JESUS IS.

[Petros, Greek], and upon this rock I will build My church; and the gates of hell shall not prevail against it" (Matthew 16:18).

This is a profound revelation. After Peter articulated the revelation of who Jesus was, he received the revelation of who he was!

Jesus used an interesting play on words here. He used two different terms for "rock." The first is *Petros*, which means "a rock or a stone." The second word is *petra*, which means "a large stone, cliff, or mountain." In other words, Jesus was saying that Peter was firm because of his revelation of who Jesus was, and the church would be established or founded on the "mountain" of the revelation of Jesus Christ.

WHAT IS IDENTITY?

Identity is defined as "the characteristics determining who or what a person or thing is." It is derived from the Latin root *idem*, meaning "same." Genesis 1:26 tells us that human beings were created in the *"image"* of God. The Hebrew word translated *"image"* is *tselem*, one of whose meanings is "resemblance." In other words, we were created to share a family resemblance with God. Of course, this is not in a physical sense, but rather in our essence—the core of who we are as spiritual beings. We resemble God in our spirit-man!

You were not created to know God from afar. You were created to know Him up close and personal. Adam's first encounter with God was face-to-face, when God breathed into his nostrils the breath of life. He wanted Adam to see Him right away when he came alive so that God would be the image all human beings would look to for their identity. God also put His Spirit inside of human beings so that we could function like Him, and He gave us a mandate to have dominion over the earth. (See Genesis 1:26.)

Thus, Adam immediately knew who he was in God and what he was created to do. Likewise, we were meant to walk in the waking consciousness of who we are in Christ. In that place, we can operate with God-confidence. Think about this for a moment. We are conscious, speaking, spiritual beings, created in the image and likeness of God. And we have the same Spirit living in us who was present at and participated in the creation of the world. Wow!

Do you know who you are? You must be able to answer this very important question. Why? Everything in your spiritual life flows from your identity. That is the very reason why the devil wants to keep people trapped in an identity crisis. If you don't know who you are, you cannot walk in the authority that comes with that identity. The devil wants us in an identity crisis because he detests the image of God, and every time he sees us, he is reminded of the Creator Himself. He tempted Adam and Eve to rebel against God, and when they succumbed, humanity was left in a fallen state in which the image of God was distorted in them. They lost their sense of identity in Him. But God had a plan of restoration.

BORN AGAIN OF INCORRUPTIBLE SEED

God was so eager to restore us to His image that He sent His own Son to die for our sins, rise triumphantly from the dead, and give His Spirit to live within us. Jesus died to take away the punishment we deserved so the Father could give us the abundant riches we did not deserve.

The Bible says that when we receive Jesus as Savior and Lord, we are "born again." What does this mean? It means that God puts His spiritual DNA inside us once more. We receive a new supernatural identity.

Jesus said, "*Verily, verily, I say to you, Except a man be born again, he cannot see the kingdom of God*" (John 3:3). Only if we are born again can we see God's kingdom. The born-again experience is indeed the entrance into the supernatural.

When we are born again, God calls us into an encounter with Himself. Until we have a personal experience with the true and living God and receive His Spirit inside us, our efforts at changing our life are merely "behavior modification." We don't see true transformation until the One who created us puts His Spirit inside us and makes us a new creation. When we become one with Christ in salvation, we enter into a new consciousness of who we are.

Therefore if any man be in Christ, he is a new creature: old things are passed away; behold, all things are become new.

—2 Corinthians 5:17

The term *"new creature"* comes from two Greek words: *kainos* and *ktisis*, which signify "a new kind of being that has been recently transformed." We become part of a new species the moment we are born again. We are "Jesus men and women." We are sons of God and joint-heirs with Jesus Christ. *"The Spirit Itself bears witness with our spirit, that we are the children of God: and if children, then heirs; heirs of God, and joint-heirs with Christ"* (Romans 8:16–17).

The rock of revelation from God is founded upon our identity in Christ. In fact, everything we do in the kingdom depends on our comprehending who we are in Christ.

As the Son of Man, Jesus was the archetype of redeemed humanity. *"God anointed Jesus of Nazareth with the Holy Ghost and with power: who went about doing good, and healing all that were oppressed of the devil; for God was with Him"* (Acts 10:38). We have been born again of incorruptible seed (see 1 Peter 1:23) by the same Spirit who raised Jesus from the dead. This means we have been born from and for the miraculous.

Thus, the supernatural is a function of our very being. We don't just "perform" the supernatural—we *are* supernatural. And the more we discover who we are in Christ, the greater the dimensions of His presence and power we are able to access. We were born—born again—for signs and wonders. Say this with me: "I am naturally supernatural!"

Behold, I and the children whom the LORD *has given me are for signs and for wonders in Israel from the* LORD *of hosts, which dwells in mount Zion.* —Isaiah 8:18

SECRET TO THE SUPERNATURAL:

MIRACLES ARE A PART OF YOUR HEAVENLY DNA. YOU

WERE BORN FOR THE MIRACULOUS!

WE ARE CHILDREN OF GOD

For most of my early life, I lived with a spirit of rejection. I never really felt accepted in my family, around my friends, or even at school. It was almost as if I were living in a glass bubble. But then I became a believer. While it would not be honest to say that all my issues vanished when I was born again, it is true that everything in my life was transformed. I began to realize the truth about who I am. I am a child of God! As simple as those words may seem, they were life-changing for me. If only each believer would truly internalize the deep meaning this truth holds! When it comes to the family of God or our heavenly citizenship, we are not illegitimate children or orphans. We are not strangers or aliens. We belong to God. And because we belong to Him, we are a part of His family. We are children of the Most High God! I don't know about you, but the thought of being a child of the most powerful Person in the universe is almost overwhelming to me.

The apostle John wrote, *"But as many as received Him, to them gave He power to become the sons of God, even to them that believe on His name"* (John 1:12). God has called us to become His sons and daughters. *"For as many as are led by the Spirit of God, they are the sons of God"* (Romans 8:14). Jesus Himself began His earthly ministry on the basis of His Sonship and identity in God. At Jesus's baptism, the Father said, *"This is My beloved Son, in whom I am well pleased"* (Matthew 3:17). You cannot access your heavenly inheritance until you understand who you are and *whose* you are.

Jesus is the elder Brother, the one entitled to the inheritance. Yet, remarkably, as God's sons and daughters, we have been made co-heirs with Jesus. Remember that the Scriptures say, *"If children, then heirs; heirs of God, and joint-heirs with Christ"* (Romans 8:17). The Father has abundantly blessed us in Christ Jesus. *"Blessed be the God and Father of our Lord Jesus Christ, who has blessed us with all spiritual blessings in heavenly places in Christ"* (Ephesians 1:3). The Psalms remind us that these benefits are available to us:

Bless the Lord, *O my soul, and forget not all His benefits.*
—Psalm 103:2

*Blessed be the Lord, who daily loads us with benefits, even the God of
our salvation.*   —Psalm 68:19

We are now in a position to expect that everything Christ has given us
will manifest in our lives, and we need to live according to our new identity
in Him. *"But put you on the Lord Jesus Christ"* (Romans 13:14).

In Romans 8:17, Paul used an interesting Greek word for *"joint-heirs,"*
which only appears once in the entire Bible. It is *synklēronomos*, which
signifies "one who obtains something assigned to himself with others; a
joint participant." This term is the combination of two words: *syn*, meaning "with," and *klēronomos*, meaning "to obtain an allotted portion (especially through sonship)." We have obtained an allotted portion in Christ
through our sonship. We walk in and release the supernatural as a part of
our inheritance and identity in Christ. This is our portion!

God, *El Shaddai*, is our all-sufficient Source of everything we need.
*"Let us therefore come boldly to the throne of grace, that we may obtain mercy,
and find grace to help in time of need"* (Hebrews 4:16). We can go beyond
that "outer court" experience with God and move deeper into the "Holy of
Holies" where God's presence is. God's children know they can come to
their Daddy *anytime*.

Please understand that your identity is different from what you do. We
must become passionate about our connection and communion with the
Father, not about the divine power itself, as important as it is for spreading
God's kingdom on earth. Jesus said to His followers:

---

*Behold, I give to you power to tread on serpents and scorpions, and
over all the power of the enemy: and nothing shall by any means hurt
you. Notwithstanding in this rejoice not, that the spirits are subject to
you; but rather rejoice, because your names are written in heaven.*
                                                        —Luke 10:19–20

ACCESSING THE INHERITANCE

Thus, miracles are part of the inheritance of the believer. They will manifest when you accept and receive who you are. Because you are *in* Christ, His power and anointing are able to flow *through* you. Don't window-shop in your relationship with God and what you need, saying, "I wish I could…" or "I wish I had…." Your Father owns the whole store! Go in and receive!

If a son shall ask bread of any of you that is a father, will he give him a stone? or if he ask a fish, will he for a fish give him a serpent? Or if he shall ask an egg, will he offer him a scorpion? If you then, being evil, know how to give good gifts to your children: how much more shall your heavenly Father give the Holy Spirit to them that ask Him?
—Luke 11:11–13

The promises, blessings, and benefits that you are ignorant of are the promises, blessings, and benefits that you are unable to receive. Satan tries to exploit our ignorance, using it as a weapon against us. God wants you to know what belongs to you, so that you can believe Him for it and receive it!

PEACE AND REST

When you lack identity, it becomes a source of confusion in your life, and confusion is the catalyst for chaos and disorder. But once you are certain of who you are as a child of God, then you can walk in peace, clarity, and confidence.

Rest in what Christ has won for you. Jesus paid for your peace of mind and heart when He died on the cross. Therefore, peace is part of your inheritance.

Let not your heart be troubled: you believe in God, believe also in Me.
—John 14:1

For God is not the author of confusion, but of peace.

—1 Corinthians 14:33

If anything in your life is in confusion, then it is not of God. Genesis 1:2 says, *"And the earth was without form, and void; and darkness was upon the face of the deep."* The term *"without form"* can also mean "confusion." When God said, *"Let there be light "* (verse 3), this signifies "Light in Me, be." Therefore, the consciousness we must walk in for our lives, as modeled by Genesis, is the separation of light from darkness and the removal of chaos.

God is light, and in Him is no darkness at all.   —1 John 1:5

And the light shines in darkness; and the darkness comprehended it not [*"has not overcome it"* NIV].   —John 1:5

Light is greater than darkness, and the darkness cannot overcome it.

In the Old Testament, when Nehemiah prayed and planned for the rebuilding of the walls of Jerusalem, he understood everything that needed to be set in order before the restoration could begin. (See Nehemiah 1–2.) Similarly, when God wants to bring change into your life, He begins by addressing the chaos and creating order. God understands the pattern necessary for bringing to pass what you have been asking Him for. Before He can do the things He wants to do in your life, there must first be order.

Many times, at first, instead of giving us a physical blessing, God will give us a word to hold on to in faith. This is the "seed form" of the answer to our request. It is up to us to cultivate what He has given us in seed form, to believe what He has spoken over our lives until it comes into manifestation. In the meantime, we are meant to occupy the place called *rest*. Don't stress, just rest! The Word is enough for the wise.

You can rest because when God speaks to you, He has already stepped into your tomorrow and seen the outcome. Once again, He is *El-Shaddai*, the all-sufficient Source of everything you need. We often become frustrated because we want God to move, not realizing He has already moved! God moves at the speed of light—His own light, which is truth. He cannot stop being God to cater to our ignorance, or what we don't know about our situation.

Paul wrote, *"Being confident of this, that he who began a good work in you will carry it on to completion until the day of Christ Jesus"* (Philippians 1:6 NIV). The reality is, in His eternal order, God sees the end from the beginning. He already finished you in eternity before He started you on earth. God's words are so powerful that the moment He speaks something into being, it is created.

For as the rain comes down, and the snow from heaven, and returns not there, but waters the earth, and makes it bring forth and bud, that it may give seed to the sower, and bread to the eater: so shall My word be that goes forth out of My mouth: it shall not return to Me void, but it shall accomplish that which I please, and it shall prosper in the thing whereto I sent it. —Isaiah 55:10–11

God has already seen the completed "you," and He has seen that it is good—not because of anything you have done, but because of His purpose and grace. The Bible says we are God's handiwork, His craftsmanship, His workmanship, *"created in Christ Jesus to do good works"* (Ephesians 2:10 NIV).

After Adam was created, Satan was terrified of him because Adam had everything that Satan didn't have: authority, dominion, and a relationship with God. And what does the believer in Christ now have? Authority, dominion, and a relationship with God! This means that devil is afraid of us, too. We don't need to be afraid of him.

FAITH

Every believer has also received a measure of faith. *"For I say, through the grace given to me, to every man that is among you, not to think of himself more highly than he ought to think; but to think soberly, according as God has dealt to every man the measure of faith"* (Romans 12:3). Christ gave you His faith as your inheritance. Faith is confidence that God will do what He says He will do. Exercise God's faith so that it can grow in you.

In Hebrews 11:6, we learn that God is a rewarder of those who diligently seek Him. He doesn't reward our sentiments or desires; He awards our pursuit. The One who made everything is *your* Daddy! You are powerful because you are filled with His Holy Spirit. Every time you release your faith, you tap in to the *dunamis* power of God. Remember, faith is the language of the supernatural.

LOVE

You must know—in your heart—the following two crucial truths if you want to live a miraculous life: 1. You are a child of God. 2. God loves you.

Miracles work by faith, but faith works by the revelation of God's love. Again, we cannot exercise faith if we don't know who God is and who we are in Him. Jesus said, *"And this is life eternal, that they might **know** You the only true God, and Jesus Christ, whom You have sent"* (John 17:3).

Eternal life begins with knowing God. This is not just head knowledge, but rather intimate, experiential knowledge. Eternal life is reflected in the Greek word *zoe*, which refers to "the God kind of life." A miraculous life begins with knowing God intimately, and thus being established in who we are in Him.

A woman who had been born with cerebral palsy came to me for prayer at a conference where I was preaching. I asked her if she wanted to be healed. Instead of laying hands on her and praying, I simply reminded her of who she was in Christ and told her that she could do all things through Christ who strengthened her. (See Philippians 4:13.) The more I made that declaration over her, the more her faith rose to the occasion. Suddenly, a woman who couldn't walk without someone supporting her was running around the entire sanctuary, shouting and giving glory to God. Hallelujah! The power of God is real, but its manifestation begins in our lives when we have a revelation of who God is and who we are in Him.

HEALING AND FREEDOM FROM BONDAGE

The more you understand who you are in Christ, the more you will recognize all that is at your disposal. You have to believe that it belongs to you. You cannot exercise authority over areas of your life or spiritual matters of which you are ignorant. Authority works by faith. You must have an understanding of these matters and the confidence in God that you have authority concerning them.

Here is the means of all your provision: you receive from your spiritual inheritance, and you live according to it. Healing and freedom are included in the inheritance that Jesus paid for on the cross. Healing is the children's bread. (See, for example, Matthew 15:22–28.) However, if we are ignorant of this provision, the devil can exercise influence and power over us in that area. *"My people are destroyed for lack of knowledge"* (Hosea 4:6). People are destroyed because of a lack of knowledge of what God has made available for them.

Remember, there are certain spiritual benefits you can't experience until you go beyond the chaos and confusion and move into who you are in God. The enemy's strategy is for you to forget what God has said, to cause you to think that He is capable of making a promise that He cannot keep. But God's Word is designed to bring us into a new consciousness, a new reality, of who we truly are.

It is the revelation of God's Word that breaks the power of ignorance! Every area of bondage in a believer's life is connected to a lie they have believed. The moment you stop believing the lie and start believing the truth according to the Scriptures, the bondage is broken.

That the God of our Lord Jesus Christ, the Father of glory, may give to you the spirit of wisdom and revelation in the knowledge of Him: the eyes of your understanding being enlightened; that ye may know what is the hope of His calling, and what the riches of the glory of His inheritance in the saints, and what is the exceeding greatness of His power to us-ward who believe, according to the working of His mighty power, which He wrought in Christ, when He raised Him from the dead, and set Him at His own right hand in the heavenly places.
—Ephesians 1:17–20

When you realize who you are and what you have access to, you will no longer be satisfied with the limitations you have embraced for your life. In the parable of the talents, the servants were held responsible for their stewardship of what they had been given. (See Matthew 25:14–30.) Ultimately, it's not what you're given, but what you do with what you're given, that matters.

If you are seeking healing, what has God promised you about it? Walk in the consciousness of your healed self. God wants you to wake up in the morning and, despite the chaos around you, say, "I am healed! Let there be light and life in my body." Walk in the greater consciousness of who you are in Christ Jesus.

AN IMPARTATION OF POWER AND VICTORY

In the book of Genesis, in the account of a man named Jacob, there is a powerful illustration of the impact of identity. The name *Jacob* means "supplanter" or "deceiver." In the Bible, names signify character, nature, purpose, and destiny. Jacob's entire life had been characterized by manipulation and deception. He manipulated his older brother out of both the birthright and the blessing, and he also manipulated his uncle Laban. He spent many years trying to live according to his own strength.

Then, one day, Jacob had an encounter with God that transformed his life forever. In his darkest hour, God visited him and asked him a profound question:

And Jacob was left alone; and there wrestled a man with him until the breaking of the day. And when He saw that He prevailed not against him, He touched the hollow of his thigh; and the hollow of Jacob's thigh was out of joint, as He wrestled with him. And He said, Let Me go, for the day breaks. And he said, I will not let You go, except You bless me. And He said to him, What is your name? And he said, Jacob. And He said, Your name shall be called no more Jacob, but Israel: for as a prince have you power with God and with men, and have prevailed.

—Genesis 32:24–28

During his struggle with the angel of the Lord, Jacob was asked, "What is your name?" In other words, "What is your character, purpose, and destiny?" Jacob answered by saying, in effect, "I am a supplanter and a deceiver!" But the angel's response was, "Your name will no longer be called Jacob, but you will be called Israel." The word *Israel* literally means "God prevails." When Jacob died to his former identity and accepted the identity God gave him, he received an impartation of power and victory. He prevailed!

When you were born again in God, you, too, experienced a name change. *"If any man be in Christ, he is a new creature: old things are passed away; behold, all things are become new"* (2 Corinthians 5:17). Consequently, you received an impartation of God's power and victory, and a new identity in Christ. The *"old man"* of sin and weakness has been done away with (see, for example, Romans 6:6) and a new creation has been born.

Power and authority flow from identity. Again, the more we realize and embrace who we are, the more the power of God will flow through us. Intimacy with God always produces miracles.

SECRET TO THE SUPERNATURAL:

THERE ARE CERTAIN SPIRITUAL BENEFITS

YOU CAN'T EXPERIENCE UNTIL YOU

KNOW AND ACT UPON WHO YOU ARE IN GOD.

PRAYER OF IDENTITY

Father, in the name of Jesus, I thank You for who You are and all that You have done in my life. I recognize that there is power in identity, and through Jesus, I have been given a new spirit and a new identity in You. I am not what I once was, but I have been cleansed from sin through the blood of Jesus and transformed by the power of the Holy Spirit. Thank You for causing me to grow in the revelation of who You are and the revelation of who I am in You. I was born for signs, wonders, and miracles, and I will walk in Your miraculous power daily. Because of the revelation of who I am in Christ, miracles and the supernatural are a common part of my life. I manifest the culture of heaven in the earth by walking in the flow of the Holy Spirit. Thank You for manifesting Your miraculous power through me. In Jesus's name, amen!

MIRACLE INSIGHTS

1. How did we define *identity*? What is the significance of knowing our identity in Christ?

2. What is the relationship between miracles and our identity as believers?

3. What does it mean to be "born again"? What took place spiritually when we were born again?

4. What does it mean to be born of "incorruptible seed"?

SCHOOL OF THE MIRACULOUS PRACTICUM

1. Everything we do in the kingdom depends upon comprehending who we are in Christ Jesus. What factors have most shaped your identity in the past? What has your perception of yourself been up to this point in your life? Write down your answers, and then write down what God says about who you are in Christ. How do they compare? Ask God to remind you of who you are in Him. Always remember that you are a child of God, and God loves you!

2. Continue to renew your mind regarding your spiritual identity by committing these verses to memory:

But as many as received Him, to them gave He power to become the sons of God, even to them that believe on His name. —John 1:12

For as many as are led by the Spirit of God, they are the sons of God. —Romans 8:14

If children, then heirs; heirs of God, and joint-heirs with Christ. —Romans 8:17

Blessed be the God and Father of our Lord Jesus Christ, who has blessed us with all spiritual blessings in heavenly places in Christ. —Ephesians 1:3

3. Miracles manifest when we accept and receive who we are in Christ. Instead of "window shopping" in your relationship with God, confidently ask your heavenly Father to provide what you need and then rest in the knowledge of His care. Remember, your Father owns the whole store. Go in and receive!

5

THE GLORY OF GOD

*"For God, who commanded the light to shine out of darkness, has
shined in our hearts, to give the light of the knowledge of the glory of
God in the face of Jesus Christ."*
—2 Corinthians 4:6

The presence in the church was so palpable that you could almost feel it with your fingers. Sounds of praise and rejoicing filled the atmosphere. Some people wept, while others lay prostrate on the floor, unable to move. Everyone saw it. Everyone felt it. It was the glory of God.

The scenario I just described occurred many years ago, and although it was not my first experience in the glory, it was definitely one of the most memorable. In fact, it happened on my birthday, while I was preaching one of my first sermons as a pastor, entitled "Grace Multiplied." I certainly don't recall anything spectacular about my preaching. Rather, what was noteworthy was the presence of God that accompanied the preaching. Because of His presence, people were touched, healed, and changed. This experience totally altered my concept of ministry and the supernatural. I understood that to see God move in our midst, we need to cultivate His presence in our churches.

Today, I believe there is a great shift coming to the church as a whole. Congregations will no longer be identified by their denominations or their religious rhetoric. They will no longer be measured by the size of their cathedrals or even the blend of coffee they serve on Sunday mornings. And they definitely will not be defined by the number of people in the congregation. In the economy of God, they will be measured by their capacity to house and properly host His presence and glory.

WHAT IS THE GLORY?

When I was growing up, I would hear people at church say, "Glory to God!" or "The glory was in that place." Honestly, I didn't quite know what they meant. Perhaps you are wondering the same thing.

What is the glory of God? As we learned in chapter 3, one of the Hebrew words translated "glory" in the Old Testament is *kabod*, which has various meanings, including "weight," "esteem," and "honor." Another way to describe the glory is "the manifest presence of God." We know that God is omnipresent, but He does not *manifest* Himself everywhere. The glory of God is the manifestation of His presence in a person or place.

We cannot separate honoring God from experiencing His presence. In fact, God will not consistently manifest Himself in a place or environment of dishonor. That is why I previously emphasized the importance of developing a culture of honor.

GOD CAME TO US!

When we read the Old Testament, it is very clear that God was not some common, ordinary, and approachable being. There are clear examples in Scripture of people being told they would die for haphazardly approaching Him.

For they could not endure that which was commanded, And if so much as a beast touch the mountain, it shall be stoned, or thrust through with a dart: and so terrible was the sight, that Moses said, I exceedingly fear and quake. —Hebrews 12:20–21

In humanity's fallen state, God is unapproachable under normal circumstances and conditions.

[God] only has immortality, dwelling in the light which no man can approach to; whom no man has seen, nor can see: to whom be honor and power everlasting. Amen. —1 Timothy 6:16

Since God dwells in unapproachable light, how could we ever approach Him? The answer is, we couldn't! Today, we are not new creations with access to God because we approached Him. We are new creations because God approached us in Jesus!

In the beginning was the Word, and the Word was with God, and the Word was God. The same was in the beginning with God. All things were made by Him; and without Him was not any thing made that was made. In Him was life; and the life was the light of men. And the light shines in darkness; and the darkness comprehended it not. There was a man sent from God, whose name was John. The same came for a witness, to bear witness of the Light [Jesus Christ], that all men through Him might believe. He was not that Light, but was sent to bear witness of that Light. That was the true Light, which lights every man that comes into the world. —John 1:1–9

In the previous chapter, we learned that God wants to be known by us, personally and intimately. He doesn't want us to see Him as a distant deity, but as a loving Father who desires to fellowship with us deeply and consistently. He desired to fellowship with us so much that He brought us into the light where He is:

But you are a chosen generation, a royal priesthood, a holy nation, a peculiar people; that you should show forth the praises of Him who has called you out of darkness into His marvelous light. —1 Peter 2:9

God not only called us out of darkness into His light, but He has also placed His light *within* us: *"Hereby know we that we dwell in Him, and He in us, because He has given us of His Spirit"* (1 John 4:13). The same Spirit who was present at creation and who raised Jesus from the dead dwells within us!

FILLED WITH GOD'S GLORY

As a believer, you are filled with the glory of God. Have you ever really considered the significance of that truth? If you embrace this reality, it will transform your life. Don't think of miracles as something you achieve or accomplish, but think of them as something you *release*. You release miracles because God's miraculous presence and power dwell within you!

One day, I was ministering in Israel at a meeting with about four hundred people in attendance. As I stood on the platform, I began to release the Word of the Lord over the congregation. The atmosphere began to shift, and people began to experience the presence of God. Why? Because I was carrying God's presence within me.

Most people have a faulty theology when it comes to approaching God and dwelling in His presence. They still believe such an experience is only for the "high priest," or certain spiritual leaders, as in the Old Testament. But in reality, Jesus is now our High Priest. He went into the heavenly

Holy of Holies once and for all to make a *"living way"* for us and to prepare a place for us in the Father's house:

> *Having therefore, brethren, boldness to enter into the holiest by the blood of Jesus, by a new and living way, which He has consecrated for us, through the veil, that is to say, His flesh; and having a high priest over the house of God; let us draw near with a true heart in full assurance of faith, having our hearts sprinkled from an evil conscience, and our bodies washed with pure water.* —Hebrews 10:19–22

More than ever, God desires to manifest His glory in and through our lives. The glory of God is the atmosphere of heaven. I want you to think about that statement. First, of all, what do I mean by "atmosphere"? In the natural world, the atmosphere is "the envelope of gases or air surrounding the earth or another planet." I am not referring to that type of environment but to a spiritual environment perceivable by the senses. One day, while in my prayer closet, I had the most miraculous experience: I saw heaven! I don't know whether this was an out-of-body experience or a vision, but it felt very real, and the first thing I noticed was heaven's atmosphere. It was very palpable. I literally felt God's presence all around me. This very "atmosphere" is what you and I carry within us by the Holy Spirit.

God exists outside of time, and therefore matters that take time on earth are accelerated in His presence. However, when we ask God to show His glory, we also need to be mindful of what we are requesting. God is holy, and we must always respect and honor Him. Note that the judgment of Ananias and Sapphira for deceiving the church and lying to the Holy Spirit was accelerated in an atmosphere of glory. (See Acts 5:1–11.)

As we have seen, it is through Jesus Christ alone that we can have an intimate relationship with God, and we know that intimacy with God produces miracles. Because the blood of Jesus has cleansed us and the Holy Spirit lives within us, we can continually abide in the presence of God.

SECRET TO THE SUPERNATURAL:

WHENEVER GOD BEGINS TO MOVE IN

ANY AREA OF YOUR LIFE,

STEWARD AND CULTIVATE IT. IN THE KINGDOM OF GOD,

WHATEVER YOU CULTIVATE GROWS.

Thus, cultivating a lifestyle of dwelling in His presence is a key component to living in the miraculous.

Not only can we continually abide in the presence of God, but His presence continually abides in us. Again, I want to reiterate the fact that you and I actually carry the atmosphere of heaven within us. This is a deep truth. You are not second class in any way. The King of Glory dwells in you by His Spirit!

THE GREATER GLORY

The heavens declare the glory of God; and the firmament shows His handywork. —Psalm 19:1

All creation declares the glory of God! Yet there is a greater manifestation of His glory on the horizon.

The glory of this latter house shall be greater than of the former, says the LORD of hosts: and in this place will I give peace, says the LORD of hosts. —Haggai 2:9

In the book of Haggai, the prophet declared that the house of God, the temple, which was being rebuilt at the time, would be more glorious than the first temple, which had been destroyed by the invading Babylonians. The rebuilding of the temple was a historical fact, but because of the life, death, and resurrection of Jesus Christ, there is a glory coming upon the house of God—not the building, but the people—that has yet to be seen.

Let me reaffirm that I believe the church is entering into the greatest time of signs, wonders, and miracles the world has ever witnessed. It will be a period of receiving supernatural manifestations of God's presence on a regular basis. In fact, I believe that miracles will become the cultural norm in the body of Christ, regardless of church denomination. We will

SECRET TO THE SUPERNATURAL:

THE MORE CONSCIOUS AND RESPECTFUL YOU ARE OF THE

PRESENCE OF GOD, THE MORE QUALIFIED YOU ARE TO

HOST THE ATMOSPHERE OF HEAVEN.

see tangible expressions of His glory in our meetings and in our communities. Living in His magnificent presence will be a daily reality for us. But we must first embrace God's glory and become people who are in love with His presence.

I am reminded of a recent outpouring of the Spirit of God in our church. Ironically, it began with the children's ministry. One of the young people in our church attended a youth camp, where they literally caught the fire of God. After attending this camp, the young person prayed over the other youth, and they were filled with the Holy Spirit. Many of them began speaking in tongues and prophesying over the entire congregation. Today, our young people flow in the prophetic consistently. We began experiencing the overflow of this glory in the general meetings attended by the adults. There were times when I couldn't preach because the presence of God was so strong. I believe such experiences will become more frequent in coming days. Men and women all over the world are going to begin to see miraculous outpourings on different levels.

GLORY-CARRIERS, ARISE!

We are called to be glory-carriers. What is a "carrier"? The English word *carrier* is defined as "a person or thing that carries, holds, or conveys something" or "a person or company that undertakes the professional conveyance of goods or people." In the natural world, a carrier of freight must deliver the goods to the client who awaits them. Additionally, a carrier will sometimes hold the freight until it is ready to be conveyed.

Consider the implications of this illustration for us: God has chosen us to convey His presence and power to other people. As His carriers, we are to release His glory everywhere we go: homes, schools, churches, banks, places of work, and much more. Wow! What an honor! Not only is this an amazing honor, but it is also a tremendous responsibility. There are people who will never receive what God intends for them unless *we* take our places as His glory-carriers. We are holding the "goods" that others need and are waiting for!

When I was in Europe several years ago, I bought an anniversary ring for my wife. The ring was expensive and precious, but the jeweler placed it in a very unassuming box. If you were to see the box, you probably wouldn't even think twice about what was in it. However, the contents of the box were significantly more valuable than the box itself. The Bible says, *"But we have this treasure in earthen vessels, that the excellency of the power may be of God, and not of us"* (2 Corinthians 4:7). You may look at yourself and think that you are unassuming or average, but the truth is, the One who lives within you is glorious! Don't be so focused on the container that you neglect its contents. It is time for the body of Christ to "open the box" and reveal the treasure within.

God is raising up a generation of glory-carriers who will be so sensitive to His presence that they will move whenever He prompts them to. The anointing of the Holy Spirit will override our man-made programs and agendas. I am talking about a time in which a Sunday morning service will go on until Monday morning. Are you ready for this? Are you prepared for a season when God purges the church so that we will be vessels of honor, prepared for His visitation? This will be more than "revival." This will be a supernatural reformation of the church as we know it. In fact, I believe it has already begun.

Always remember that you are "holding" someone's heavenly encounter inside of you. Certainly, God can manifest Himself to people without using human agencies, but He usually chooses to employ His followers for this purpose. In fact, almost every miracle in the Bible involves the employment of a human agency. We are God's agents. We are His ambassadors!

The world around us is awaiting the release of what the Father has placed within each one of His children by His Spirit. A young man in our church had a skin condition that caused his face and head to become discolored. But as he attended the church and began to experience the power and presence of God, his skin condition cleared up supernaturally! Hallelujah!

The glory of God dwells inside of you. The miracle power of God dwells inside of you. So, the next time you go to work, school, or church, say, "The glorious presence of God dwells within me. I release this presence to flow out of me to those who need an encounter with God!"

PRAYER FOR THE MANIFESTATION OF GOD'S GLORY

Father, in the name of Jesus, I thank You for Your mighty power and presence working in and through my life. Your Word says, *"We have this treasure in earthen vessels, that the excellency of the power may be of God, and not of us."* Therefore, I declare that I am a glory-carrier! I hold Your glory within me through the Holy Spirit, and I am transformed by Your presence and power. I recognize that I am carrying the miracle that someone is waiting to experience. Father, please bring me into a greater consciousness of this truth. Awaken my spirit to the reality of Your presence in my life. By faith, I release the glory of God to those in my sphere of influence. I am not only a carrier of Your glorious presence, but I am also a benefactor of Your glory within me and upon me. I desire to be a part of the great awakening that You are releasing upon this generation. I make every part of my life available for Your glory. In the name of Jesus, amen!

MIRACLE INSIGHTS

1. What is the Bible referring to when it talks about the "glory of God"?

2. What does it mean to be a glory-carrier?

3. We talked about the "greater glory" coming to the earth. What is the greater glory? What will it be characterized by?

4. What is the difference between how God's people experienced the glory of God in the Old Testament and how believers experienced His glory in the New Testament?

MIRACLE TESTIMONIES

MIRACLES OF BLESSING AND HEALING

J. reported, "I was listening to you on [Sid Roth's television program *It's Supernatural!*], speaking about getting into the presence of the Lord, and you said you start by singing the song "This Is the Air I Breathe." You prayed afterward for viewers, and as you were praying, I felt a heavy coolness being poured over my head. It was like oil being poured over me, but the coolness was like water. I gave God all the glory for the blessing I received.

———

Several years ago, my wife started to work out at the gym. She would get up every morning and make sure she got her workout in. Then, one day while she was at the gym, she severely injured her right arm and was in so much pain that she couldn't lift her arm to do anything. My wife thought it would be fine in a few days, but three days later, the pain was still excruciating. She made a trip to emergency room but was told they couldn't treat her because she was pregnant. She went home, and I prayed over her from midnight until three in the morning. At three, I felt led to anoint her with oil and rebuke the injury. My wife said the pain decreased immediately. By noon, she barely felt any pain. When the orthopedic surgeon's office called to schedule her appointment, she told them, "I don't need you anymore! I am healed." Glory to God!

6

THE POWER OF A RENEWED MIND

"And be not conformed to this world: but be you transformed by the renewing of your mind, that you may prove what is that good, and acceptable, and perfect, will of God."
—Romans 12:2

When I was growing up, one of my favorite TV cartoons was *The Transformers*. It was about alien robots who could assume the structure and shape of any machine they scanned. They became whatever they gazed upon. In a much more profound way, we experience a process of spiritual and mental transformation when we continually gaze upon the Lord:

But we all, with open face beholding as in a glass the glory of the Lord, are changed into the same image from glory to glory, even as by the Spirit of the Lord. —2 Corinthians 3:18

After years of preaching and teaching the uncompromised Word of God, I have come to the conclusion that there is almost nothing more significant than the supernatural power of a transformed mind. The Bible tells us not to be conformed to the world. The Greek word rendered "*conformed*" in Romans 12:2 means "to conform one's self (i.e. one's mind and character) to another's pattern, (fashion one's self according to)." The English word *conform* comes from the Latin term *conformare*, which means "to make something like another."

We are commanded not to take on the shape of the world, but to take on a higher form by renewing our mind. Like those "extraterrestrial" transformers, we, too, are "not of this world" and must be transformed if we want to operate in miracles and live a supernatural lifestyle. (See, for example, John 17:14; 18:36.) Simply put, if you want to experience God on a greater level, you must change the way you think!

WHAT CONTROLS YOU?

Why is change so necessary in this process? I'm glad you asked!

Love not the world, neither the things that are in the world. If any man love the world, the love of the Father is not in him. For all that is in the world, the lust of the flesh, and the lust of the eyes, and the pride of life, is not of the Father, but is of the world. —1 John 2:15–16

When the Bible says, "*Love not the world,*" this isn't a reference to the physical planet or the people in it, but rather to the fallen world system that operates on the earth. This system is governed by "*the lust of the flesh, and the lust of the eyes, and the pride of life.*" Let me be clear: to love the world is not just to participate in sinful activities, such as illicit sex, drugs, or violence. It also includes possessing a "worldly" mind-set. To think like the world and embrace its ideas is just as much loving the world as committing any of the "big" sins we can conceive of.

We must understand how the human senses operate under the influence of the sinful nature. The *"lust of the flesh"* refers to a preoccupation with being gratified by what we can feel or experience. The *"lust of the eyes"* is an unwholesome desire to have the things that we see. The *"pride of life"* is basically vanity. All of these amount to an obsession with, and deification of, the natural senses.

The reality is, sin has conditioned the human race to be preoccupied with our five human senses—sight, hearing, smell, taste, and touch. Yet, when we were born again, we were delivered from being governed by our senses. The senses are God-given and are good and beneficial in themselves, but they are often influenced by the sinful nature, and we were never meant to be controlled by them. We were meant to be governed and controlled by the Spirit of God.

This is why it is vital for us to be transformed. The kingdom of God is governed by a totally different system of rules and regulations than the world is. If we want to function supernaturally, we must be transformed in our priorities and thinking. In the Greek, the word for *"transformed"* in Romans 12:2 is *metamorphoo*, meaning "to metamorphose," "to transform," or "to change into another form." Again, note that we are to change forms. This is not a physical transformation (although physical change can be good), but rather a spiritual transformation.

"Be you transformed by the renewing of your mind." Our thoughts are powerful. The Bible tells us, *"For as* [a person] *thinks in his heart, so is he"* (Proverbs 23:7). Our thoughts influence every area of our lives, prompting our attitudes and actions. In order to manifest the will and plan of God, we must embrace a spiritual mind-set.

SECRETS OF A SPIRITUAL MIND

For to be carnally minded is death; but to be spiritually minded is life and peace. —Romans 8:6

God will not manifest Himself in a way that runs contrary to the Bible because He and His Word are one. (See John 1:1–2.) Thus, a spiritual outlook based on God's Word and the work of His Spirit is essential for releasing heaven on earth. We already possess the mind of Christ by virtue of the indwelling Holy Spirit (see 1 Corinthians 2:16), but we must learn to yield to the mind of Christ daily. This requires us to actively challenge any thoughts that are not in alignment with the Word of God.

Often, it is uncomfortable (and sometimes offensive to us) to confront our wrong thinking. Whenever I teach on the supernatural, it never fails that some people reject the instruction, not because it is unscriptural, but because it goes counter to their personal experiences and patterns of thinking. Can you see the problem with this perspective? The Bible talks about miracles from Genesis to Revelation. Furthermore, millions of people all over the world are experiencing supernatural encounters with God. If the Bible clearly reveals a reality that is intended for believers, but it is not manifest in your life, it means your life needs adjustment. You can never base your theology solely on your personal experiences. Yet the more we grow spiritually, our personal experiences should be a reflection of sound theology.

Do you see why it is so important for us to renew our mind? When you think about it, our mentality affects every area of our lives, including the spiritual aspect. What would happen if we learned to live our lives according to the mind of Christ? What would happen if His thoughts became our thoughts? How would this change the fabric of our spiritual experience? Every time we renew our mind, we gain access to greater dimensions of God's glory and power!

Imagine for a moment a caterpillar. It spends the early part of its life crawling on the ground, eating leaves. Then, one day, it surrounds itself with a cocoon so that it can undergo metamorphosis. While in this protective case, it begins to change into a different type of insect. After the process is complete, it emerges from the cocoon as a butterfly. Now it can fly! The potential to be a butterfly was latent until the transformation took place. The same is true of you and me. Like the caterpillar, we must undergo a transformation to release the full potential that God has placed within us. The renewal of our minds is the catalyst for this supernatural transformation in our lives. The difference between a "caterpillar Christian" and a "butterfly Christian" is the way they think.

DEVELOPING A MIRACLE PARADIGM

People frequently become frustrated over the fact that the healings, deliverances, and other breakthroughs they read about in the Bible are not evident in their own lives. The problem often exists within our paradigm. A *paradigm* can be defined as "a pattern or model" or "a worldview underlying the theories and methodology of a particular scientific subject." The Scriptures clearly articulate the place and necessity of miracles in the kingdom paradigm. So, why do so many people struggle with believing and operating in the miraculous?

But if our gospel be hidden, it is hidden to them that are lost: in whom the god of this world hath blinded the minds of them which believe not, lest the light of the glorious gospel of Christ, who is the image of God, should shine to them. —2 Corinthians 4:3–4

The Scripture says that *"the god of this world"* has blinded the minds of those who do not believe. The word for *"blinded"* here signifies "to blunt the mental discernment," or "to darken the mind." This means that the enemy of our souls has deliberately deceived many people and blinded them to the miraculous power and efficacy of the gospel of Jesus Christ. Earlier, I used the term "gospel of exclusion," indicating the fact that so many people are excluding the power of God from their presentation of the gospel. Remember, the gospel hinges on the most supernatural event in the history of the human race: the resurrection of Jesus by the glory of the Father. That resurrection was a miracle! It is only sound to believe that our faith is based on the miraculous power of God in incarnating His Son and raising Him from the dead.

Being a Christian without believing and operating in the miraculous is like being a fish that will not swim. Yet the only fish that don't swim are dead fish. I don't know about you, but I have no desire to be a "dead" Christian!

We must develop a miracle paradigm. This is a spiritual framework that positions us to walk in and release miracles *daily*. Do you expect to see miracles in your life and the lives of others every day? Do you anticipate the move of God everywhere you go? Your paradigm affects your capacity. You must set aside anything that hinders you from receiving your supernatural inheritance.

There was a precious couple who got ahold of my teaching on the supernatural. They had attended church their entire lives, but once they began to renew their mind with the Word of God concerning who God is and who they are, everything shifted. They began boldly praying for people and seeing miraculous results. For example, they prayed for a man who had been seriously wounded and placed in an induced coma, and the man was healed supernaturally. Hallelujah! Thousands of people all over the world are being equipped in the school of the miraculous to release God's powerful presence in their lives and the lives of those around them. Glory to God!

DO YOU BELIEVE?

If we are going to flow in the miraculous presence and power of God daily, we must believe that this lifestyle is available to us, and then release our faith to see, receive, and walk in it. Herein lies the challenge! Many Christians suffer from a "disease" (a *dis-ease*) named *unbelief*. Others actually have a stronghold of unbelief in their lives.

In the New Testament, one of the Greek words for unbelief is *apistia*, among whose meanings are "unfaithfulness," "disobedience," and "weakness of faith." When a person is operating in unbelief, they are not walking in biblical faith or they are suffering from a weakness of faith. One synonym for *unbelief* is *disbelief*. Think about unbelief as a mental and spiritual framework that is contrary to the Word of God. Sometimes, our unbelief is a result of what we have been taught or what we haven't been taught. This is why sound doctrine is vital when it comes to the miraculous. How can people believe in miracles when they are taught that miracles do not exist?

Recently, I watched a seminary-trained pastor teach his congregation of thousands that they have no power over the devil, Satan is stronger than they are, and they ought to "respect the devil." Can you imagine that? How can people walk victoriously in spiritual warfare if they believe this kind of teaching? They can't! While we should recognize that Satan has power and not be casual about it (see verse 9 of Jude), we must also acknowledge that the power of God is infinitely greater! *"Greater is He that is in you, than he that is in the world"* (1 John 4:4). If we are going to see different results spiritually, then we must change our mental and spiritual framework.

When I encourage people to believe God, they often have a very defensive reaction. I hear responses like, "Oh, I believe with all my heart! Are you trying to say I don't have faith?" Have you ever heard someone say something like that? Have you ever said it? But the question remains: Do you really believe God? Once more, belief is demonstrated by actions and not just words. It doesn't matter what we say if our actions contradict that claim. If someone told you they were the best financial planner in the world, but you found out they had loads of debt and were experiencing financial ruin, would you sign up for their financial course? Probably not, right? Why? Because their results weren't in alignment with what they claimed. Belief is an action word. Anytime we change our belief system, it will result in a change in our actions.

Again, I want to be clear that every born-again Christian has faith! If you didn't have faith, you wouldn't be saved. Remember that God has given every believer a *"measure of faith"*:

For I say, through the grace given to me, to every man that is among you, not to think of himself more highly than he ought to think; but to think soberly, according as God has dealt to every man the measure of faith. —Romans 12:3

In essence, doubting God's power is not about the absence of faith, but rather the presence of unbelief. We have noted that when the Bible speaks of unbelief, it is referring to a way of thinking and reasoning that is diametrically opposed to the Word of God. The apostle Paul wrote,

(For the weapons of our warfare are not carnal [natural], *but mighty through God to the pulling down* [demolishing] *of strong holds;) casting down imaginations, and every high thing that exalts itself against the knowledge of God, and bringing into captivity every thought to the obedience of Christ.*   —2 Corinthians 10:4–5

Paul asserted that we must pull down strongholds and cast down imaginations and "*every high thing that exalts itself against the knowledge of God.*" What is he referring to?

The Greek word translated "*imaginations*" is *logismos*, which can indicate "a reasoning: such as is hostile to the Christian faith"—and to God's Word. These "imaginations" are like cases against the Word of God in the courtroom of your mind. They are the insidious thoughts and suggestions from the enemy that tell you what God "can't" do. Such thoughts are the foundation of the stronghold of unbelief. Our thoughts, past experiences, and circumstances can create a mental fortress that the enemy occupies and exploits to keep us from the life God intended for us.

There is only one way to deal with these mental fortresses of doubt and unbelief: demolish them with the Word of God by faith!

THE DIFFERENCE BETWEEN *FAITH* AND *BELIEVE*

We having the same spirit of faith, according as it is written, I believed, and therefore have I spoken; we also believe, and therefore speak.
                    —2 Corinthians 4:13

Let's begin by reviewing what we know about faith:

1. *"Faith is the substance of things hoped for"* from the unseen spiritual realm. (See Hebrews 11:1.)

2. Faith is the evidence that gives substance to what we believe. (See Hebrews 11:1)

3. Faith responds to the revelation of God's Word "in the now," or today.

It is important to understand the difference between the words *faith* and *believe*:

- *Faith* is a noun, while *believe* is a verb.

- If believing is like credit, then faith is like the currency that backs the credit.

Every time we read, speak, and meditate on the Word of God, we are renovating our mind and shifting our paradigm. "To believe" means not only to accept something as true, but also to act accordingly. Jesus said, *"He that believes on Me, the works that I do shall he do also; and greater works than these shall he do; because I go to My Father"* (John 14:12).

As believers, we are called to do the works that Jesus did—and even greater works, by His power within us. Do you really believe that? The proof is in the actions you take.

Action activates miracles. The first time I prayed for someone with cancer, I had to press through my fear, doubt, and unbelief. I had to go beyond the arguments in my head that told me there was no way this person would be healed. I prayed anyway! The moment I made a conscious decision to believe the Word of God over doubt, something supernatural happened: the person was healed.

What if someone is not healed? Keep believing! Remember, believing is a conscious decision. You can't believe by accident. I made a decision to believe that the Word of God was more powerful than cancer. We often say that "seeing is believing," but in actuality, "believing is seeing." Until you believe, you won't see the glory of God! Our focus should never be,

SECRET TO THE SUPERNATURAL:

CONSISTENTLY MEDITATING ON GOD'S WORD

TEARS DOWN THE WALLS OF FEAR, SKEPTICISM,

CYNICISM, AND DOUBT IN YOUR MIND.

"What if they don't get healed?" Rather, it should be on God's Word: *"He that believes on Me...."*

I related a testimony in my book *Invading the Heavens* that I think is a perfect illustration of how action activates miracles. I was in a meeting in which I prayed for a woman who had just experienced a stroke, causing her to lose the use of her right arm and her ability to speak. Because I was a man of great faith and power, I called her forward and declared that she was healed. Guess what happened after I prayed for her? Absolutely nothing! This was actually quite embarrassing for me, because I was focusing on myself instead of the Lord. In that moment, I realized that God wanted me to take my eyes off of myself and put my faith and confidence in Him. So, I continued to press in to the miracle.

All of a sudden, another level of faith rose up inside me. I told the woman to take the microphone that I was holding. The woman's friend told me that she couldn't grab the microphone because she was unable to use her arm due to the stroke. But God gave me boldness, so I insisted that the woman grab the microphone from my hand. Her friend actually became angry with me at that point, but I still insisted. As I continued to believe and press in to the miracle, something shifted in the spiritual atmosphere. The woman's faith began to rise up! Suddenly, she snatched the microphone from my hand and shouted, "JESUS!" Remember, she had not been able to speak since her stroke. Glory to God! The power of God touched this woman, and she was healed supernaturally! What would have happened if I had settled for the fact that nothing occurred the first time I prayed?

Our responsibility is to believe the Word of God, and God's responsibility is to manifest His power. If you will do the believing, He will do the manifesting. Hallelujah!

PRAYER FOR THE RENEWAL OF YOUR MIND

Father, in the name of Jesus, I thank You for Your presence and miraculous power in my life. Your Word commands us to be transformed by the renewing of our mind. Therefore, I declare that my mind is renewed by the Word of God. I possess the mind of Christ. I think differently! Nothing is impossible to me because I am a believer and not a doubter! As I renew my mind through Your Word, strongholds of fear and unbelief are demolished by the power of Your Spirit. I believe in miracles! I will manifest the supernatural power of God in my life. I refuse to be a slave to fear, doubt, cowardice, or timidity. I press into miraculous breakthroughs by the persistent practice of believing Your Word and doing what it says, no matter what! Thank You, Father, for the promises of Your Word in my life. In Jesus's name, amen!

MIRACLE INSIGHTS

1. What does the Bible mean when it says, *"Be you transformed by the renewing of your mind"* (Romans 12:2)?

2. How can we be sure that every believer has faith?

3. What is the difference between *faith* and *believe?*

4. What is meant by the term "miracle paradigm"? How do we develop a miracle paradigm?

SCHOOL OF THE MIRACULOUS PRACTICUM

1. The renewal of our minds is the catalyst for supernatural transformation in our lives. Our thoughts, past experiences, and circumstances can create a negative mental fortress that keeps us from the life God intends for us. Begin to develop a miracle paradigm by writing down areas in your life where you are operating in unbelief about seeing God move in the miraculous. Then, next to them, list corresponding Scripture passages that will renew your mind in those areas. Focus on these Scripture passages for an entire month, asking God to change your mind-set.

2. As you go about your day, whenever you have a thought or a process of reasoning that is opposed to the Word of God, stop and consider what you are thinking. Then, actively bring that thought into captivity to the obedience of Christ. (See 2 Corinthians 10:4–5.)

3. Action activates miracles. Remember this promise from Jesus: *"He that believes on Me, the works that I do shall he do also; and greater works than these shall he do; because I go to My Father"* (John 14:12). We have learned that faith is like currency, while believing is like credit. What person or circumstance will you pray for today, making a conscious decision to believe the Word of God rather than allow doubt and uncertainty to take over? Begin a journal to track your prayers for God's intervention, as well as His answers and miraculous manifestations.

7

THE AUTHORITY OF PROCLAMATION

"You shall also decree a thing, and it shall be established to you."
—Job 22:28

Along with the supernatural power of a transformed mind, nothing has been more effective in my walk with the Lord than *proclaiming* God's Word. What do I mean by this? I'm so glad you asked!

A *proclamation* can be defined as "a clear declaration of something" or "a public or official announcement dealing with a matter of great importance." In the second definition, I want you to pay close attention to the word *official*. This term indicates that a proclamation is not given randomly or offhandedly, but is in fact planned and could have legal ramifications.

For example, In 1863, in the midst of a bloody civil war, United States president Abraham Lincoln issued a proclamation that "'all persons held as slaves' within the rebellious states 'are, and henceforward shall be free.'"[2] This was a statement from someone who had the legal authority to issue the

---

2. See https://www.archives.gov/exhibits/featured-documents/emancipation-proclamation.

proclamation. As a result, the words of the proclamation could be enforced. It became (technically) illegal to hold individuals as slaves in states that had seceded from the Union. (By the end of 1865, the thirteenth amendment was ratified, abolishing slavery in the entire country.)

Moreover, in the natural realm, under a full monarchy, when a king made a proclamation, it became law. We are God's kings and priests (see Revelation 1:6; 5:10), and when we make a declaration in line with His will, spiritually speaking, it becomes "law." When our words are aligned with the Word of God, they have "legal" authority in the spiritual realm.

WE ARE A SPIRITUAL LEGISLATURE

The concept of spiritual authority connected to our words should not be foreign to those of us who are members of the body of Christ. In Matthew 16:18, Jesus that He would build His church. The Greek word translated "*church*," *ekklesia*, comes from a political term, one of whose meanings is "an assembly of the people convened at the public place of the council for the purpose of deliberating." It is derived from the compound words *ek* and *kaleo*, which literally mean "called out."

Think about a legislative body for a moment. The members have policy discussions and make "proclamations," or bills, and these bills become laws when enough of the legislators agree on them, and they are passed. A similar process occurs in the spiritual realm. As we join together with God and His Word, whatever we bind on earth is bound in heaven (deemed unlawful) and whatever is loosed on earth is loosed in heaven (deemed lawful). (See Matthew 18:18.) Every born again believer has spiritual legislative authority in the kingdom of God.

Years ago, when I was in college, I didn't have a car. My previous vehicle had been flooded, and it was totaled. I didn't have any extra money and had very little credit to buy another car. Consequently, I had to walk about five miles from my apartment to the college and back. Constantly making this trek was very exhausting. There came a point when I was sick and tired of being sick and tired. One night, while walking home, I said, "I'm getting a car this week!" By faith, I was so convinced of this fact that I spoke those words and believed them. Within a week's time, I had purchased a new car. I don't know how I purchased it! I just remember catching a ride to a car dealership one day and coming home with a new car. In the past, when I had applied for credit at a car dealership, I had been denied. But there was something different this time! I hadn't realized that my words carried so much weight in the spiritual realm.

In another instance some years later, my wife and I were ministering at an Assemblies of God church. Among the people who came to the altar for prayer was a precious woman who had melanoma, or skin cancer. As I was about to lay hands on her and pray, I heard these words by the Holy Spirit: "Don't lay hands on her. Proclaim that she shall not die but live and declare the works of the Lord!" (See Psalm 118:17.) I followed those instructions and made that faith-filled proclamation over the woman. As I spoke, the presence and power of God came upon her, and she fell to the floor. Minutes later, she got up, feeling lighter and refreshed. She thanked me for praying for her and told me that she felt the presence of God. Forty-eight hours later, this woman contacted us and told us that the cancerous growths had fallen off her body. She was healed! Hallelujah!

What happened? By the direction of God's Spirit, I proclaimed the Word of God over her life and body. After I made that declaration, a miracle took place.

I must warn you that this works both ways. Negative words can also have legal implications in the spiritual realm. This is especially true for those who are in a position of authority. For example, as a pastor, I must be mindful of the things that I speak over my congregation. As a parent, I must be mindful of what I speak over my children. Speaking negative words over people and situations can have an adverse affect on them. We will talk more about this shortly.

THE REALITY OF THE SPIRITUAL REALM

The spiritual realm is a deeper reality than the natural realm. If we would really grasp this truth, it would change our lives.

SECRET TO THE SUPERNATURAL:

WHAT YOU SAY HAS A TANGIBLE EFFECT ON THE

ATMOSPHERE AROUND YOU.

SPEAKING GOD'S WORD CREATES AN

ATMOSPHERE FOR MIRACLES.

Through faith we understand that the worlds were framed by the word of God, so that things which are seen were not made of things which do appear. —Hebrews 11:3

The Message Bible puts it this way:

By faith, we see the world called into existence by God's word, what we see created by what we don't see.

Notice that the Bible says *"the worlds were framed,"* or set into proper order, by the words God spoke. Because we have been created in the very image and likeness of God, we are meant to manifest His nature. God is a spiritual Being who governs by what He says, and we were created by Him to govern on earth through our words. The entire universe was brought into order by divine proclamations from God! Amazing! When God wanted light, He spoke it into existence. Likewise, if we want miracles, we have to speak them into manifestation.

Your words indeed shape your world. That is why operating in the supernatural power of God requires an understanding of the power of proclamation. At every juncture of transformation in my spiritual life, I have made a faith-filled proclamation. I can remember deciding one day that I wanted to operate in signs and wonders, so I said out loud, "I will see miracles manifest in my life!" And I saw exactly that! You may be thinking, "Is it really that simple?" My answer is, "Yes!" I challenge you to persistently proclaim God's Word over your life and watch the outcome. You must keep speaking the Word of God over and over again! Keep speaking God's Word until you see the manifestation.

INSTRUMENTS OF CONSTRUCTION OR DESTRUCTION

The Bible is very clear about the effect of our words:

Death and life are in the power of the tongue: and they that love it shall eat the fruit thereof. —Proverbs 18:21

What does this verse mean? The Hebrew word translated as *"power"* is *yad*, which literally means "hand." Death and life are in the "hand" of your tongue. A physical hand can be an instrument of construction, but it can also be a weapon of destruction. It depends on how a person uses it. The same is true of the tongue. Our words can either build or destroy. As we have learned, our words carry legal authority in the realm of the Spirit. This means that our words give license to matters and situations in our lives. Many Christians do not realize the profound power of their words. If they did, they probably wouldn't speak half the things they say on a regular basis!

We must be careful what we give license to by what we say or proclaim. During one of my ministry trips to Africa, I became very ill, exhibiting all the symptoms of cholera. When I came back to the States, I had one of the worse cases of diarrhea in my life. (Please forgive the imagery.) The problem was, I was in the middle of taping a television show that I was launching. I didn't feel I had time to go to the doctor, and the over-the-counter medication wasn't working. I was going to the bathroom fifteen to twenty times each hour, and I became seriously dehydrated. (On the bright side, I lost a lot of weight and it made me look great on camera!)

Interestingly, the more I proclaimed that I had cholera, the worse it became. You would think that I would know better, right? One night, while I was in my room praying, I heard the Lord say, "How long are you going to tolerate this?" Initially, I was perplexed by this question. But then I realized that God was calling me to action. I needed to speak something that would shift the atmosphere. Finally, I mustered the strength to say, "In the name of Jesus, I take authority over this spirit of infirmity that is attacking my body! I command my body to be healed!" That was it! Shortly afterward, I went to sleep. The next day, the cholera-like symptoms disappeared. Hallelujah! What changed? My words changed!

What have you given license to with your words? What situation or circumstance has been prolonged by what you have been speaking? You may need to take inventory of your words. I want to reiterate the fact that, as you begin to change what you say, it is not about speaking some "magic words," but it is about consistently speaking faith-filled words that will make all the difference.

"SPEAK THE WORD ONLY"

In the book of Matthew, there is an account of a centurion who had a profound encounter with Jesus because he recognized the place of authority in proclamation:

> And when Jesus was entered into Capernaum, there came to Him a centurion, beseeching Him, and saying, Lord, my servant lies at home sick of the palsy, grievously tormented. And Jesus says to him, I will come and heal him. The centurion answered and said, Lord, I am not worthy that You should come under my roof: but speak the word only, and my servant shall be healed. For I am a man under authority, having soldiers under me: and I say to this man, Go, and he goes; and to another, Come, and he comes; and to my servant, Do this, and he does it.
> —Matthew 8:5–9

This centurion understood the power of words spoken with authority. As a man of authority himself, and as a man under authority, he recognized that when a king made a declaration, it was so. Therefore, when he approached Jesus, with complete faith in His authority, he knew that the Lord only needed to say the word and his servant would be healed. "And Jesus said to the centurion, Go your way; and as you have believed, so be it done to you. And his servant was healed in the selfsame hour" (verse 13).

If you and I are going to experience God's miraculous power, we must make a daily habit of proclaiming the Word of God and making statements of faith. Often, when I wake up, I say, "Miracles are happening for me today!" or "Something good is going to happen to me and for me today!" As simple as these statements are, they have the power to shift the trajectory of my entire day. As Cindy Trimm puts it, "You must command your morning." We must be intentional about how each one of our days is going to look.

You might be saying, "I thought that God determined the outcome of my day." Wrong! Although the Lord is sovereign, we determine to what extent we will enjoy His promises and blessings in any given day. We must deliberately embrace the miraculous daily. Nothing just happens by some sort of spiritual osmosis or because God "willeth it"! Again, to experience the miraculous in your life, you must be intentional. I call this "prophetic intentionality." When you learn to live in a state of intentionality, constantly anticipating that God will move, you will consistently live in the miraculous. Every day, you must decide that you are going to experience a miracle.

One of the keys to living in prophetic intentionality and expectancy is prayer. Intercession postures our heart in a state of expectancy. The spirit of expectancy is indeed the catalyst for miracles. Miracles don't just happen for those who need them, but for those who expect them.

OPERATING IN HEAVENLY AUTHORITY

Another powerful biblical illustration of the influence of proclamation on the spiritual and physical world is found in the book of Matthew:

And when [Jesus] was entered into a ship, His disciples followed Him. And, behold, there arose a great tempest in the sea, insomuch that the ship was covered with the waves: but He was asleep. And His disciples came to Him, and awoke Him, saying, Lord, save us: we perish. And He says to them, Why are you fearful, O you of little faith? Then He arose, and rebuked the winds and the sea; and there was a great calm. But the men marveled, saying, What manner of man is this, that even the winds and the sea obey Him! —Matthew 8:23–27

When confronted by a storm, the disciples responded with fear and dread, but Jesus responded by rebuking the winds and the waves. The Greek word translated *"rebuked"* is *epitimao*, whose meanings include "to reprove" and "to censure severely." It can also have the sense of a formal legal ruling regarding the inappropriate actions of an offender. In other words, Jesus issued a legal statement against the storm, and the storm had to obey the proclamation.

The implication in the text is that the disciples had the capacity to take the same action Jesus did, in faith and under His authority. Our words can carry heavenly authority!

Many times, we focus on trying to change things physically. But in the spiritual realm, change begins with what we think and what we say. When we ask God for something and attempt to accomplish it through our own ability, we confine the answer to the prison of our self-effort. God doesn't need our help. What He desires is our faith and obedience to His Word.

Every time we make a proclamation by faith, in alignment with the Word, we are setting spiritual forces into motion that will ultimately manifest in our lives. If you want your life to change, stop complaining and start proclaiming! Begin by making the following declarations, based on Deuteronomy 28:13 and 2 Timothy 2:21:

I am the head and not the tail.

I am above only and not beneath.

I am blessed in every area of my life.

I am a vessel of honor, fit for God's use.

I am full of supernatural power and grace.

I am a vessel of the miraculous.

SECRET TO THE SUPERNATURAL:

EVERY TIME YOU PROCLAIM THE WORD OF GOD IN FAITH,

YOU CONFORM YOUR WORLD TO GOD'S WORD.

THE MORE YOU PROCLAIM,

THE MORE YOUR LIFE WILL REFLECT HEAVEN.

PRAYER TO RELEASE MIRACLES

Father, in the name of Jesus, I thank You for who You are and all that You continue to do in my life. Your Word declares that You created the universe with Your words. I recognize the profound power of Your words, including the supernatural power of proclaiming Your Word from my mouth daily. I recognize that speaking Your Word can shift the atmosphere and release miracles. Therefore, through the power of proclaiming, I release Your miracle power right now. People are healed when I speak Your Word. Chains are broken when I speak Your Word. Your glory is revealed when I speak Your Word. Thank You for teaching me how to guard the words of my mouth. I know that miracles will be my new normal, every day of my life. In the name of Jesus, amen!

MIRACLE INSIGHTS

1. What does the term *proclamation* refer to? What is unique about proclaiming compared with any other form of speaking?

2. What effect do our words have on the spiritual atmosphere around us?

3. What are the spiritual implications of Matthew 18:18: *"Verily I say to you, Whatsoever you shall bind on earth shall be bound in heaven: and whatsoever you shall loose on earth shall be loosed in heaven"*?

4. Why isn't it usually enough to make a declaration once?

MIRACLE TESTIMONIES

MIRACULOUS FINANCIAL FAVOR

In obedience to God, my wife and I sowed into others' lives and paid people's rents and mortgages, and within a month, God blessed us with supernatural provision and a new car. Even the car salesman said he had never seen anyone receive such favor. The miracle of favor continues to overwhelm our ministry. As we have sown into good ground, we have seen a supernatural harvest time and time again.

Sister C. wrote to us, "We searched high and low for the owner of a rental home who would accept our application to rent. We tried over four applications, but no one would say yes because our circumstances are a little untraditional. We sowed a seed in church last Sunday and arrived home to a yes application. We are moving in to our new home today."

MIRACULOUS PROVISION FOR DEBT

Several years ago, the Lord impressed upon my heart to take my congregation through a series of prophetic prayers regarding debt cancellation. I told them that within thirty days, many would experience a supernatural cancellation of their debt. One such individual was a young lady who received a phone call from her parents, who informed her that an account had been opened in her name when she was a baby and that this account had matured and was available for making withdrawals. The next day, she went to the bank and made a withdrawal from the account that covered all of her debts. I believe God is releasing financial miracles all over the earth today! Are you ready to receive a financial miracle? Are you ready for your debts to be canceled supernaturally?

8

RELEASING THE SUPERNATURAL

"From [Paul's] body were brought to the sick handkerchiefs or aprons,
and the diseases departed from them,
and the evil spirits went out of them."
—Acts 19:12

Strutting around the platform with her tiny frame and peculiar accent, she stopped abruptly and, with a stern face, shouted, "Don't grieve the Holy Spirit! Don't you know He's all I got?" These were the words of the late healing evangelist Kathryn Kuhlman. I never had the privilege of seeing her in person, but on a number of occasions, I have watched video recordings of her preaching. Sister Kathryn Kuhlman is a spiritual hero to me. From a distance, she has discipled me on the necessity of "the anointing." If we are going to experience miracles daily, we need to understand the secrets to operating supernaturally, and the anointing is another significant facet of living a supernatural lifestyle.

THE ANOINTED ONE AND HIS ANOINTING

God anointed Jesus of Nazareth with the Holy Ghost and with power: who went about doing good, and healing all that were oppressed of the devil; for God was with Him. —Acts 10:38

When the Bible speaks of the anointing, it is talking about the dynamic, yoke-destroying, burden-removing, supernatural power of God that operates within every believer. We must fully realize this fact: everything Jesus did while He was on the earth, He did as the Son of Man, anointed by the Holy Spirit. He did not operate as deity, even though He was fully God as well as fully man. The good news is that, as believers, we have the same anointing residing within and resting upon us!

But the anointing which you have received of Him abides in you, and you need not that any man teach you: but as the same anointing teaches you of all things, and is truth, and is no lie, and even as it has taught you, you shall abide in Him. —1 John 2:27

Many Christians do not understand the fundamentals of yielding to and operating in the anointing. First of all, we must recognize that the Anointed One (Jesus) and His anointing truly abide in us. Remember, the same Spirit who raised Jesus from the dead dwells within us. The term "Christ" is not Jesus's last name, but rather means "anointed." He is the Source from which all heavenly anointing flows. When we yield to Him, we yield to His anointing—the power of God working in and through us.

The Scriptures often depict the anointing as oil. (See, for example, Psalm 89:20–21; James 5:14–15.) The Greek word translated *"anointing"* in 1 John 2:7 means "an unguent or smearing, i.e. the special endowment ("chrism") of the Holy Spirit." In biblical times, fragrant oil would be poured on the priests' heads, signifying the call of God upon their lives.

You recognized the priests not only by their garments, but also by their aroma of oil.

In a similar way, because we are kings and priests to God through Jesus Christ (see Revelation 1:6; 5:10), we are anointed and carry the aroma of heaven. This "oil" destroys yokes and removes burdens, not only in our lives, but also in the lives of the people with whom we come into contact.

THE ANOINTING IS TANGIBLE AND TRANSFERABLE

What are the main characteristics of God's anointing?

1. The anointing is tangible.

2. The anointing is transferable.

First, the anointing is tangible in that it can often be felt or sensed. We see this in the biblical account of the woman with the flow of blood:

*And a certain woman, which had an issue of blood twelve years, and had suffered many things of many physicians, and had spent all that she had, and was nothing bettered, but rather grew worse, when she had heard of Jesus, came in the press behind, and touched His garment. For she said, If I may touch but His clothes, I shall be whole. And immediately the fountain of her blood was dried up; and she felt in her body that she was healed of that plague. And Jesus, **immediately knowing in Himself that virtue had gone out of Him**, turned Him about in the press, and said, Who touched My clothes?* —Mark 5:25–30*

In this instance, the *"virtue,"* or anointing, was tangible because Jesus felt it going out from His body. In another biblical example, the power of the Lord was *"present to heal"*:

And it came to pass on a certain day, as [Jesus] was teaching, that there were Pharisees and doctors of the law sitting by, which were come

> *out of every town of Galilee, and Judaea, and Jerusalem: and the power*
> *of the Lord was present to heal them.* —Luke 5:17

This is another case of the tangible, *dunamis* power of God (the anointing) operating in a specific atmosphere. Countless times, I have felt the anointing come upon me while I was preaching or teaching the Word of God. In addition, I can't tell you how many times, when someone has laid hands on me, I have felt the anointing flow through them to me. It's awesome! However, I want you to understand that the anointing is more than a feeling. Some people relegate the anointing to a feeling and thus misunderstand its essence. You may not *feel* anointed, but you are! The anointing abides within you regardless of how you feel.

The second aspect of the anointing is that it is transferable. This means it can be conveyed from one person or thing to another person or thing. For example, in Mark 5, when the virtue went forth from Jesus to the woman with the issue of blood, the healing anointing transferred from His body to her body. Another biblical illustration of the transferable nature of the anointing is the case in which people received healing through items that had been worn by the apostle Paul:

> *And God wrought special miracles by the hands of Paul: so that from*
> *his body were brought to the sick handkerchiefs or aprons, and the dis-*
> *eases departed from them, and the evil spirits went out of them.*
> —Acts 19:11–12

Imagine cloths that were exposed to the anointing on Paul's life being used to minister healing to the sick and deliverance to those who were demon-possessed! Why did this occur? Because the anointing is transferable. I have received numerous testimonies from people who told me that they felt the anointing and received healing or deliverance while reading my books.

Am I saying that even books can carry the anointing of God? Absolutely! So can programs on television. In fact, I was born again while watching a prerecorded message from a well-known pastor and TV evangelist. Even though the show had been taped at a previous time, it still carried God's anointing. Let me ask you this: if a piece of cloth, a book, or a television program can carry the presence of God, what makes you think you can't?

I remember a particular instance during one of my television broadcasts when the Lord gave me a word of knowledge for a specific person, and I prayed for them. Later on, I received a communication that this person had experienced the presence of God while they were watching the broadcast in their living room. The individual was set free from demonic powers and filled with the Holy Spirit. Glory to God! The more you understand the anointing, the more you will begin to operate in it.

YOU ARE ANOINTED!

A common misconception among believers is that only certain "special" individuals in the church are anointed by God, but the "average" Christian is not. First of all, there is no such thing as an average believer! If the Spirit of God lives in you, then you are extraordinary. You are anointed! The key is to activate and release that anointing through faith and obedience. The moment you obey the assignment God has placed upon your life is the moment you will see the manifestation of the anointing in and through you. For example, Jesus instructed us:

Go you therefore, and teach all nations, baptizing them in the name of the Father, and of the Son, and of the Holy Ghost: teaching them to observe all things whatsoever I have commanded you: and, lo, I am with you always, even to the end of the world.

—Matthew 28:19–20

You won't experience the anointing to evangelize if you don't share your faith. You won't experience the anointing to preach if you never open

SECRET TO THE SUPERNATURAL:

IF YOU WANT TO SEE A MIRACULOUS DISPLAY

OF GOD'S POWER, ACT ON HIS WORD IN FAITH,

REGARDLESS OF HOW YOU FEEL.

your mouth to present the gospel. You activate the anointing by *acting on God's Word.*

Again, every time you act on a divine instruction, the anointing is released. You don't need more anointing. You just need to release what you already have!

When you see Christian leaders doing great exploits in the name of Jesus, you are witnessing something that you have the same potential—perhaps even greater potential—to walk in. This is what Paul meant in his epistle to the Philippians when he said, *"I can do all things through Christ which strengthens me"* (Philippians 4:13).

Remember, it is the Anointed One and His anointing that give us strength within. It is the anointing that enables us to operate in the miraculous power of God. The more we are aware of the anointing *within* us, the more yielded we will be to the anointing flowing *through* us!

Let me repeat: You don't need more anointing. You need to release the anointing you already have! However, remember that the manifestation of the anointing can increase when you learn how to place a demand on it. Earlier, we talked about the necessity of honor as it relates to living a supernatural lifestyle. What you honor, you often attract. The more you respect the anointing upon your life and the lives of other men and women of God, the more the anointing upon your life will increase.

THE MYSTERY OF ELIJAH'S MANTLE

You may be familiar with the story of the prophets Elijah and Elisha. The relationship between these two servants of God is an excellent illustration of the power of the anointing. God told Elijah to train Elisha as his replacement. When Elijah's tenure in ministry was about to come to a close, Elisha asked his mentor for a double portion of his anointing. Elijah told Elisha that if he saw him when he went up to God in the fiery chariot, he could have what he asked for. And that is what happened. Then, Elisha took up Elijah's mantle and began to operate in miracles. (See 2 Kings 2:9–15.) This is what I call the Law of Proximity. In order to receive an anointing from Elijah, Elisha had to be in proximity to that anointing.

SECRET TO THE SUPERNATURAL:

GET CLOSE TO THE ANOINTING THAT

YOU WANT TO RECEIVE.

Thus, the first aspect of the mystery of Elijah's mantle is the Law of Proximity. Connecting to an anointing on someone else's life (through books, teachings, and relationships) can increase the anointing on your life. The anointing is caught, not taught. You cannot teach someone how to be anointed, but a person can increase in the anointing through impartation. In the book of Romans, the apostle Paul spoke of impartation:

For I long to see you, that I may impart to you some spiritual gift, to the end you may be established. —Romans 1:11

Paul was writing to the church in Rome, informing them of his desire to release an impartation to them that would establish them spiritually. *Metadidomi* is the Greek word translated *"impart."* It comes from two words: *meta*, among whose meanings is "with," and *didomi*, which can mean "to give something to someone" or "to give to one [who is] asking." This implies that the transfer of gifting or anointing happens through connection. So again, one of the keys to receiving, increasing, and walking in the anointing is a connection with another believer.

Elisha had to stay connected with Elijah if he wanted to receive a double portion of the anointing his mentor had. This biblical principle of connection is a challenge for us in the transient and individualistic Western culture of our day. Many people don't stay connected to anyone or anything long enough to receive what God has for them. Because Elisha understood the importance of connection, he remained connected to Elijah until the very end.

I remember receiving a particular notification on my phone that a download was available for updating my device. When I went into my settings to download the update, the phone informed me that this download required a Wi-Fi connection, and the phone also had to be plugged into a power source. Without the connection, the download would remain available to me, but the transmission could not be completed. Similarly, if you want to operate in the anointing and live in the miraculous, you must remain "connected" and "plugged in" to the Power Source, which is the Holy Spirit. Even though God is omnipresent, we can draw closer to Him through intentional actions. Meditate on His Word, pray, and stay connected to other believers in a life-giving community.

The second aspect of the mystery of Elijah's mantle is the Law of Surrender. Let's review what "surrender" means in a spiritual sense. In the natural world, surrender means "to stop resisting…an enemy or opponent and submit to their authority." However, for the purpose of this book, we are using surrender in the context of yielding to God and ceasing to resist Him. God is not our enemy but our Friend. When it comes to the anointing of the Holy Spirit, we must learn how to yield to Him, submitting to His power and authority. Spiritual power is increased through our surrender and submission to God.

PRAYER OF ANOINTING

Father, in the name of Jesus of Nazareth, I thank You for who You are and Your precious anointing. Your Word says that the anointing destroys the yoke and removes heavy burdens. I recognize that the anointing I have received from You abides in me and is truth. I also recognize that the Holy Spirit within me is the Power Source of any and all anointing. I declare that Your power and presence in my life increase because I surrender to You in obedient submission to Your Word. As I yield to Your Word and Spirit, I release the supernatural in my life. I am anointed to operate in signs, wonders, and miracles. As I remain connected to the Anointed One and His anointing, chains are broken off of my life and the lives of those around me. I receive a supernatural impartation from You to see miracles in my life daily. I am anointed to see a move of God in my life. In Jesus's name, amen!

MIRACLE INSIGHTS

1. What is the biblical definition of "the anointing"?

2. Who would you consider anointed? What makes them anointed?

3. Can the anointing increase in a person's life? If so, how?

4. With regard to the "mystery of Elijah's mantle," what are the two spiritual laws that cause a person to increase in the anointing?

MIRACLE TESTIMONY

One day, a young lady in my church came to me and said, "Pastor, I want a double portion of the anointing that's on your life." As new covenant believers, with the Holy Spirit living within us, I don't believe we need to ask anyone for a double portion, but I do believe that God desires that we all increase in the anointing daily. So, I prayed for her that God would give her the desire of her heart. When I prayed for this precious woman, she fell under the power of God and was filled with the Holy Spirit. From that day forward, she began to walk in signs and wonders. Every time I saw her, she had another testimony of a miracle that had recently taken place. Hallelujah! She was willing to humble herself and submit to my spiritual authority. Some people would be too proud to make such a request.

SCHOOL OF THE MIRACULOUS PRACTICUM

1. Read the following portions of Scripture, keeping in mind that whenever Jesus acted on earth, He did not operate as deity but as the Son of Man, anointed by the Holy Spirit: Matthew 14:13–21; Luke 8. Then, remind yourself that you have the same anointing residing within and resting upon you!

2. Perhaps you don't "feel "anointed. What does the Word of God say about this in 1 John 2:27? How will you allow God's truth to change your perspective on your anointing?

3. You have been anointed by God to destroy oppressive yokes and remove burdens. Begin to live in the power of the Anointed One and His anointing. Ask God to use you as a vessel to transfer His supernatural power to people and situations in need of a miracle. Begin by sharing your faith with someone else and allowing God to work from there.

9

BREAKING THE STRONGHOLD OF FEAR

"Fear you not; for I am with you: be not dismayed; for I am your God: I will strengthen you; yea, I will help you; yea, I will uphold you with the right hand of My righteousness."
—Isaiah 41:10

I am no stranger to fear. In fact, when I was young, I was absolutely terrified to speak in front of people. I would literally start crying every time I had to do a presentation before a crowd. Today, I spend most of my time in front of large groups, whether in the pulpit or speaking on television. In chapter 1, I said that I believe God has a sense of humor. The way He is using me in public ministry today is another piece of evidence to support that claim! It seems ironic that the very activity I was terrified of doing as a child is what I do best as an adult. God can overcome all our fears, to His glory! *"To the intent that now to the principalities and powers in heavenly places might be known by the church the manifold wisdom of God"* (Ephesians 3:10).

WHAT IS FEAR?

What is fear, and why is it an important topic in relation to living miraculously? I'm glad you asked! Fear hinders us from becoming all that God wants us to be. It manifests in many ways, including bashfulness, insecurity, timidity, feelings of intimidation, nervousness, anxiety, and a paralyzing incapacity. Satan's agenda is to use fear to manipulate and control us, corrupt our perception and thinking processes, and keep us trapped in his deceptions so we cannot live in the power of God. He wants us to succumb to lies and intimidating statements like the following:

+ God can't use me!

+ I am not spiritual enough.

+ I am too shy and afraid to step out in faith.

+ My sinful past has disqualified me from being used by God in a mighty way.

+ If I walk in the miraculous, I will be rejected by my peers.

+ God can only use people who have a large television ministry.

+ God won't answer my prayers.

Such lies are often fueled by doubts like these:

+ What if I pray for someone and they don't get healed?

+ What if my expectations are disappointed?

+ What if I look foolish?

GOD'S PERFECT LOVE CASTS OUT FEAR

"There is no fear in love; but perfect love casts out fear: because fear has torment. He that fears is not made perfect in love" (1 John 4:18). The Greek word translated *"fear"* in this verse is *phobos*, meaning "fear, dread, terror" or "that which strikes terror." It is the word from which we derive the English term *phobia*—an irrational fear of something or someone. Some people are afraid of spiders, and this is called *arachnophobia*. Others are afraid of closed spaces, and this is called *claustrophobia*. In every instance of a

phobia, there is an irrational belief that distorts reality. The truth is, in certain cases, a spider or a closed space might harm a person, but overall, the likelihood is very low. Yet when someone has a phobia, they believe something that doesn't really have the potency or probability of affecting them negatively will do just that.

The Bible says that there is no fear in love. We cannot be in fear and faith at the same time because faith works by love. (See Galatians 5:6.) If you are going to live a miraculous life, you must conquer fear. Two thousand years ago, Jesus triumphed over fear on the cross, and we must appropriate His victory today in our lives. *Phobos* fear is based on a lie because it is contrary to the Word of God. Fear is motivated by what we think, see, or hear. Faith is motivated by what God says!

FALSE EVIDENCE

When we fear, we accept "evidence" that appears real but is false. And by operating in fear, we are placing our belief and expectation in something destructive.

Let me be clear: there are natural fears. For example, if someone jumps out of the bushes and runs toward you with a knife, it is natural to be alarmed, leading to a "fight or flight" response of self-preservation. I am not saying that we won't ever find ourselves in a genuinely difficult or even dangerous situation. Such circumstances can occur, and they are real. However, even then, God's love and faith can replace our fear with trust in His presence, power, and protection.

But there are also many unnatural fears, even if they have some basis in reality, such as a fear of rejection, fear of failure, fear of abandonment, or fear of exposure. It is critical that we recognize the difference between natural and unnatural fears. It is also important to note that remaining in a state of fear is unnatural. We should never continue in any negative state for a prolonged period of time because it can have a damaging effect on us spiritually, emotionally, mentally, or physically. We were not created for fear and worry!

STRONGHOLDS OF FEAR

In God have I put my trust: I will not be afraid what man can do to me. —Psalm 56:11

I know by experience that it is nearly impossible to exercise spiritual authority while simultaneously operating in fear. There was a time in my life when I couldn't worship God freely because I was afraid of the way I would look to other people. I was unnaturally self-conscious, and I was worried that people would think I was "weird" if I worshipped God unreservedly. Because of this mind-set, I was harboring a fear of man.

The fear of man brings a snare: but whoso puts his trust in the LORD *shall be safe.* —Proverbs 29:25

By obsessing over an imagined reaction of the people around me, I opened my life to fear, which in turn brought a level of bondage with it. At first, I didn't know that I was actually in bondage as a result of making an idol out of other people's opinions of me. But one day, I decided that I would no longer embrace the lie that negative reactions to my worship style—whether real or imagined—mattered. Immediately, I began to worship God freely, and I have been free in my worship ever since.

In one form or another, many people live in bondage to the stronghold of fear. To become free of fear's grip, it is essential to understand what a "stronghold" is. In the natural world, a stronghold is "a place that has been fortified so as to protect it against attack." Strongholds are often used by armies during warfare. In the spiritual world, it is much the same, except that these fortresses are occupied by demonic powers. The devil establishes strongholds in people's lives so he can steal their joy and rob them of the purpose and plan of God. But these strongholds have vulnerabilities, and we need to understand what they are so we can defeat the enemy's schemes.

We can break down demonic fortresses in our lives through God's superior weapons. Satan's strongholds cannot stand up against the truth of God's Word and the power of His Spirit.

Let's return to a passage that we looked at in chapter 6, "The Power of a Renewed Mind":

> (For the weapons of our warfare are not carnal [natural], but mighty through God to the pulling down [demolishing] of strong holds;) casting down imaginations, and every high thing that exalts itself against the knowledge of God, and bringing into captivity every thought to the obedience of Christ. —2 Corinthians 10:4–5

We have learned that the Greek word translated "imaginations" is logismos, which can indicate "a reasoning: such as is hostile to the Christian faith"—and to God's Word. The enemy of our soul uses deceitful arguments and false images to erect strongholds in our spiritual life. But God is raising up a generation of people who will break the stronghold of fear and insecurity and will move into the sphere of power and influence that God has ordained for them.

FREEDOM FROM THE SPIRIT OF FEAR

I vividly remember a time during the early days of my Christian life when I was tormented at night while I slept. This went on for quite some time. Honestly, I didn't know what to do. Every time I would fall sleep, a demonic attack would ensue. To me, it was reminiscent of an epileptic seizure, because I would experience moments of total paralysis. It was absolutely terrifying. It came to the point where I didn't want to go to sleep anymore.

One night, the demonic attack came, as usual, but this time, I decided that enough was enough. Even though I felt like I was being suffocated to death, I mustered the strength to yell, "Jesus!" Suddenly, there was a release and then a calm. In that moment, I understood—not just intellectually, but experientially—that I had no more reason to be afraid of the devil. I was set free from the spirit of fear.

Yes, fear is definitely a spirit, and like all spirits, it must bow to the authority of the name of Jesus! If you are going to walk in the miraculous power of God and operate in signs and wonders consistently and effectively, you need to rid yourself of an attitude of fear! You must be confident of God's power within you. *"Greater is He that is in you, than he that is in the world"* (1 John 4:4).

I have heard it said, "Do it afraid!" But it is my personal conviction that we should "do away with fear." Why? Fear torments. It is better to not be afraid!

DO NOT BE AFRAID!

There are many places in the Bible that encourage us not to be afraid. Fear paralyzes us, preventing us from living the abundant and miraculous life God wants for us. Furthermore, *phobos* fear can sometimes become a self-fulfilling prophecy, aiding the manifestation of the very thing of which we are afraid. Whatever we fear, we facilitate! Just as faith facilitates the miraculous power of God, fear facilitates the destructive power of the enemy. As flies are attracted to open containers of food, demonic forces are drawn to fear.

Just as with phobias in the natural world, every area of bondage in a believer's life is connected to a lie they have believed—about God, themselves, or their circumstances. Once the lie is broken, the bondage is released. The devil wants to keep many people trapped in fear because if they continue to believe lies about themselves or others, they will remain in a place of stagnation or become further weakened in their faith. Jesus calls us beyond the place of fear into the place of faith, where we are empowered to live supernaturally. *"For you have not received the spirit of bondage again to fear; but you have received the Spirit of adoption, whereby we cry, Abba, Father"* (Romans 8:15).

IT'S NOT IN YOUR NATURE

Have you ever heard someone use the expression "We're only human"? Actually, nothing could be further from the truth. If you are born again, you are, in a sense, more than just human. You have been given the gift of the Holy Spirit. In other words, you literally have the nature of God inside of you. Is God fearful? No! God is not fearful, and neither should you be.

For God has not given us the spirit of fear; but of power, and of love, and of a sound mind. —2 Timothy 1:7

The Greek word translated *"fear"* in this verse is also the term for "timidity" or "cowardice." It is clear that fear can quench the manifestation of the supernatural. To see the power of God demonstrated in your life, you cannot be timid. You must be willing to take risks. There are certain spiritual blessings and manifestations that you will never experience until you take a risk. What you desire is beyond the threshold of fear. Often, people will pray for a certain experience or manifestation from God, but they want to remain in their comfort zone, which can include any place of spiritual stagnation. We have to move out of our comfort zone.

You and I were designed to be full of faith! We are meant to live in a continual state of expectation about what God will do next. We are meant to live in anticipation of good things happening in our lives. The nature of our born-again spirit is faith and power, not fear and paralysis.

CONFRONT YOUR FEAR

I have found that fear requires confrontation. Many times, people haven't fully recognized the fear that has been controlling them. Once they identify it, they must be willing to challenge it. Again, it is fear that tells us things such as, "What if I pray for this person and they don't get healed?" One day, I was praying for a woman who was blind in her right eye. I said all of the right things and had all of the right outward expressions of faith, but in my heart, although I didn't recognize it, I was afraid. I was ministering

SECRET TO THE SUPERNATURAL:

CONFRONT THE VERY THING YOU FEAR.

ONCE YOU CONFRONT THE FEAR,

IT WILL LOSE ITS POWER.

to this woman in a meeting where there were forty thousand people in attendance, and the service was also being recorded. I was thinking, "What if she doesn't get healed? People are going to think I am a charlatan!" Right? Wrong! The burden of manifestation doesn't rest upon us. The burden of belief rests upon us, but the burden of manifestation rests upon God alone.

Well, that precious woman was not healed. Later that night, I asked God, "Was it her lack of faith?" God spoke to me very clearly and said, "It wasn't her lack of faith. It was yours!" I was taken aback by that statement! It was then that I realized I had been operating in the spirit of fear. I learned a very valuable lesson that day, one that I stated earlier in this chapter: fear and faith cannot operate in the same space. After the Lord corrected me in this area, I changed my perspective, and I saw many blind people healed. In fact, eye conditions of all sorts are often healed in my meetings.

Walking in the supernatural power of God requires boldness and audacity, which are the opposite of fearfulness. Every time we take a step of faith, we are positioned to experience a greater expression of God's power. Faith is the necessary ingredient to overcoming the power of fear. Faith leads to action, and action activates miracles!

The truth is, there is no need to fear that God won't come through in a particular situation. God is faithful and His Word is absolutely true. It doesn't matter what a circumstance looks like. Stay in faith, and you will see the manifestation.

Another form of fear that plagues many believers is the fear of inadequacy. They don't think they have what it takes to operate in miracles. Perhaps you feel this way or know someone else who does. Hundreds of thousands of Christians all over the world are living beneath their miraculous potential because they are looking at what they perceive to be a great limitation—themselves. I understand because, at one point, I didn't realize that I was a major mountain standing in between me and the life God had for me. However, quite simply, it's not about us! One of the keys to seeing miracles happen in your life is getting over "self." If you will take your eyes off of yourself and place them on your Creator, things will drastically shift in your life. I encourage you to do a work for the kingdom of God that you have never done before. Step out in a tangible and measurable way today! Don't worry about your past or your problems. Just tell God, "I am available to You! Do a miracle through my life in the power of Your Spirit."

PRAYER FOR DELIVERANCE FROM FEAR

Father, in the name of Jesus, I thank You that You are love, and that You are the God of love. There is no fear in love because perfect love casts out fear. Thank You for the Spirit of faith and confidence in Your Word. I refuse to submit to the power of fear! Through faith in Your Word, I demolish the stronghold of fear in my life and in the lives of others. I take authority over the spirit of fear. I have not received a spirit of fear but a spirit of power, love, and a sound mind. Therefore, I will never be afraid to take a risk when I know You are leading me to step out in faith. I live a life of fearless faith and boldness. Thank You for removing the residue of fear, guilt, and shame from my life. Through the authority of Your Word, I make fear bow. Thank You for delivering me from the spirit of timidity, cowardice, and self-consciousness. In the name of Jesus, amen!

MIRACLE INSIGHTS

1. What role does fear potentially play in hindering the miraculous power of God from working in your life?

2. What is the difference between rational and irrational fears?

3. Name three of the major fears that Christians have regarding the idea of God operating through them.

4. How do we overcome fear in our life?

MIRACLE TESTIMONIES

A MIRACLE OF CONCEPTION

A couple in our church had not been able to conceive a child for many years. After much prayer and no results, they had become quite frustrated with the situation. They came to us and asked us to pray for "the fruit of the womb." Within several months, the wife conceived, and she gave birth to a beautiful, healthy baby. Glory to God!

SUPERNATURAL CHILDBIRTH

If you know my wife and me, you know that we are no strangers to childbirth. (We now have five children.) After my first two children, I think we became experts. However, God began to show us a more excellent way when it came to faith and miracles. This was especially relevant to giving birth to children. Trust me, I am well aware that my wife is the one who gave birth to all of our children, and not me, as the nurse would so eloquently remind me. But God was shifting us! My wife got hold of a teaching on supernatural childbirth. She learned that she didn't have to settle for what family members or programs on television say childbirth has to be. We realized that pain in childbearing was a function of the curse. My wife made up her mind that it was not God's will for her to suffer in the delivery room. She declared that the curse upon Eve was not applicable to her, and she has experienced supernatural deliveries with little to no pain. In fact, my son came out so fast that the midwife had to catch him by the leg! If I hadn't been in the delivery room, I probably wouldn't have believed it myself. After the delivery, the midwife and staff told us that it was the most amazing birth they had ever seen. Hallelujah!

10

THE SPIRIT OF AWAKENING

"Wherefore He says, Awake you that sleep, and arise from the dead,
and Christ shall give you light."
—Ephesians 5:14

I have said this before, and I will say it again: a great spiritual awakening is coming in the earth. It will be like nothing we have ever seen before. It will not be like the revivals of old. Many Christians have the idea that revival will be coming down from heaven, but that's not exactly the case. "Revival" has already come down from heaven. The church was birthed nearly two thousand years ago when the Holy Spirit descended from heaven on the day of Pentecost to dwell in and upon believers. This means that the life of heaven is even now with us. Glory to God!

Peter, standing up with the eleven, lifted up his voice, and said to them,
You men of Judaea, and all you that dwell at Jerusalem, be this known
to you, and hearken to my words: for these are not drunken, as you

suppose, seeing it is but the third hour of the day. But this is that which was spoken by the prophet Joel; And it shall come to pass in the last days, says God, I will pour out of My Spirit upon all flesh: and your sons and your daughters shall prophesy, and your young men shall see visions, and your old men shall dream dreams: and on My servants and on My handmaidens I will pour out in those days of My Spirit; and they shall prophesy: and I will show wonders in heaven above, and signs in the earth beneath; blood, and fire, and vapor of smoke.

—Acts 2:14–19

Peter was quoting from the book of Joel when he said, "*I will pour out of My Spirit upon all flesh….*" (See Joel 2:28.) The question is, if the Holy Spirit was poured out nearly two thousand years ago, and the Spirit lives within us, why is the church still waiting for the Spirit to be poured out? Please don't get me wrong. I believe that we should intercede for a move of the Spirit in our land, but I don't believe it's coming "down." This next great move of God is coming from within—within *us*! It's not coming down; it's coming out! Did you hear what I just said? The church is pregnant with revival, waiting for the waters of the Spirit to break in this generation.

RIVERS OF LIVING WATER

For a long time, the church of the Lord Jesus Christ has been asleep. Yes, we have had spurts of revival and breakthrough over the years, but these jolts of miraculous power were intended to do more than excite us; they were meant to awaken the church so that we could move in the divine purpose of God. Unfortunately, we have often built shrines around the instruments of revival rather than seeking the One who revives us.

What do I mean by this? Many Christians like to talk about revivalists from earlier times and even locations of revivals. Some make pilgrimages to these sites. It is good to remember, appreciate, and learn from past revivals, but the danger is in staying there. God never intended for the catalyst for revival to become a campsite. Moreover, revival was never meant to be a relic of the past that we talk about as if it were some isolated historical event; revival was always meant to be a means to an end—the spiritual awakening of the church.

Ephesians 5:14 says, *"Awake you that sleep, and arise from the dead...."* The Greek word translated *"awake"* is *egeiro*, among whose meanings is "to arouse from sleep, to awake," "to arouse from the sleep of death, to recall the dead to life," and "to cause to rise from a seat or bed." Interestingly, it is the same word Jesus used when He said to the paralyzed man at the pool of Bethesda, *"Rise, take up your bed, and walk"* (John 5:8). Jesus commanded a man to arise after he had been bedridden for thirty-eight years! He was not calling this man to physical healing alone, but also to spiritual and personal awakening. (See verse 14.)

One of the definitions of *awakening* in *Merriam-Webster's* dictionary is "a coming into awareness." It is time for the church to come into awareness! What are we to come into an awareness of? An awareness of who we are in Christ and of the Spirit who resides within us.

He that believes on Me, as the scripture has said, out of his belly ["innermost being" NASB] *shall flow rivers of living water.*
—John 7:38

It was always God's design that the Holy Spirit would flow from the believer's innermost being. We were never intended to be like a shallow lake or stagnant pond, but a living river. The word *"rivers"* in the above verse signifies a torrential flow of water. A mighty river is meant to flow out of our spirits into the world around us. This torrent is powerful enough to move mountains of obstacles and reshape the culture around us. Just as the might and power of natural waves and storm surges are capable of flooding entire cities, God desires to flood cities and nations with the culture of His kingdom—a culture of awakening and reformation.

SECRET TO THE SUPERNATURAL:

GOD IS THE FIRST; HE IS SELF-EXISTENT,

SELF-SUSTAINING, AND SELF-AWARE,

KNOWING THAT EVERYTHING HE DOES IS GOOD.

WALKING IN THE CONSCIOUSNESS OF GOD

The Bible records, *"And the LORD God formed man of the dust of the ground, and breathed into his nostrils the breath of life; and man became a living soul"* (Genesis 2:7). I want you to think about this fact for a moment: the Lord God breathed into Adam's nostrils. This means that man was created and brought to life through a face-to-face encounter with God. I believe that when God gave the breath of life to Adam, He also breathed the Holy Spirit into him. This would mean that the first conscious experience Adam had was to look into the face of his Creator and be filled with His presence.

All human beings were meant to have face-to-face encounters with God and to be filled with Him! The Bible indicates that it was customary for Adam and Eve to walk with God in the cool of the day. (See Genesis 3:8.) This reveals that they had an intimate relationship with Him. It was always God's intent to have a personal and intimate relationship with each member of humanity.

And God said, Let Us make man in Our image, after Our likeness: and let them have dominion over the fish of the sea, and over the fowl of the air, and over the cattle, and over all the earth, and over every creeping thing that creeps upon the earth. So God created man in His own image, in the image of God created He him; male and female created He them. And God blessed them, and God said to them, Be fruitful, and multiply, and replenish the earth, and subdue it: and have dominion over the fish of the sea, and over the fowl of the air, and over every living thing that moves upon the earth. —Genesis 1:26–27

We were designed to have dominion over the earth in the context of intimacy with and obedience to God. It was the Creator's plan for the human race to fill the earth so that earth could look like heaven. What does this fact have to do with miracles and the church? Great question! If we are going to see the power of God flow through us, we must understand,

SECRET TO THE SUPERNATURAL:

YOUR CONSCIOUSNESS DETERMINES YOUR LEVEL

OF AWARENESS, AND YOUR LEVEL OF AWARENESS

DETERMINES YOUR LEVEL OF AWAKENING.

in a deep way, His original design and purpose for creating us. If we don't know what God intended in the garden of Eden, we won't know why Jesus came and what His sacrifice restored to us. Furthermore, we won't understand why miracles are important in establishing God's new covenant in Christ on the earth.

In Genesis 3, we learn that Adam and Eve believed the lie of Satan and disobeyed God by eating the fruit of the Tree of Knowledge of Good and Evil. As a result, the entire human race became spiritually separated from God—we lost the glory and intimacy with Him that we once had. This glory and relationship with God is what Jesus came to restore. Receiving and living in this restoration is the key to a supernatural life. God wants us to fill the earth with the presence of heaven and drive out the hell that has been operating in the world since the fall of man. Satan's usurped authority in the world ended with Jesus's victory on the cross. As believers, we are part of God's plan to restore His kingdom on earth in the power of Christ.

GOD-CONSCIOUSNESS VERSUS SELF-CONSCIOUSNESS

As I mentioned previously, one definition of *awakening* is "a coming into awareness." Awareness refers to consciousness. For the purposes of this book, we will focus on two types of consciousness: God-consciousness and self-consciousness. Before I explain these two dynamics, I think it would be helpful to tell you about some of my experiences with the presence of God.

In the summer of 1996, I was a zealous young Christian, adamant about receiving everything God had for me. I asked God for the baptism in the Holy Spirit, and when I received the baptism, my life was radically transformed. I immediately began to have supernatural encounters with God. Some of these encounters were so significant that they permanently changed the way I saw my heavenly Father. He was more than just a distant deity whom I learned about in Bible study. He was real; He was substantial. *He loved me!*

The first types of supernatural encounters I experienced were prophetic utterances and words of knowledge. These communications from God are

SECRET TO THE SUPERNATURAL:

STAND FIRM ON THE WORD OF GOD,

REGARDLESS OF WHETHER PEOPLE AGREE WITH YOU!

among the gifts of the Spirit that Paul writes about in 1 Corinthians 12. God began showing me information and insights about people (myself included) and about the church globally, and I would speak out prophetic words in church. It was amazing!

However, when I shared with some friends in my local church about what God was doing, they questioned whether I was going crazy. They cautioned that I should not go off the deep end. What was interesting is that everything I shared with them was fully biblical. Sadly, very few of those friends are in ministry today. You will come to realize that the supernatural may seem strange to some people, even believers. But strange is not the same as unscriptural. We must learn not to be discouraged by the negative opinions of others, particularly when those opinions are in opposition to the Word of God.

The more I prayed in the Spirit and meditated on the Word of God, the more I became aware of and sensitive to God's presence. It was as if I was literally walking with God. This is what I call "God-consciousness." I learned to walk in the reality of the heavenly realm daily. I wasn't worried about my needs, frailties, or failures; I was simply basking in God's presence every day.

The second type of supernatural encounter I had was angelic visitations. That's right! I began sensing and seeing angels. I vividly remember a particular encounter in which I met an angel at a bus stop. I saw a man who looked very peculiar, in the sense that I could not place his ethnicity. He looked like all the tribes of the earth in one. This man asked me to tell him the time, and then he vanished into thin air! I looked everywhere and could not find him. I knew in my spirit that I had "entertained" an angelic being:

Be not forgetful to entertain strangers: for thereby some have entertained angels unawares. —Hebrews 13:2

After I became deeply involved in my local church, I began to notice other people reacting negatively to my spiritual life. Some would persecute

SECRET TO THE SUPERNATURAL:

GLOBAL REVIVAL STARTS WITH PERSONAL REVIVAL.

THE TRANSFORMATION OF CULTURE BEGINS WITH THE

TRANSFORMATION OF CHARACTER.

me and make negative comments, such as, "You are so heavenly minded, you are no earthly good." Others would refer to me with criticism as "preacher man."

These reactions caused me to ask myself if I was trying too hard spiritually. I wondered if maybe it didn't really take all of the effort and sacrifice I put into developing my relationship with God. Slowly, but surely, as I entertained these thoughts, I became more focused on my frailties and failures than I was on God. I became more concerned about people's opinions than I was about Him. This is what I mean by "self-consciousness." Many believers are walking in self-consciousness. Of course, we should make an effort to be pleasing to God in our everyday lives, which often involves examining our motives and attitudes, but we should not be more self-conscious than we are God-conscious.

One of the enemy's devices is to get believers to become so self-absorbed that they are no longer aware of the presence of God in their lives. Ultimately, self-consciousness leads to sin-consciousness, in which we emphasize our sins, failures, and frailties more than we do God Himself. Make no mistake: self-consciousness is a form of idolatry. We cannot serve two masters!

PERSONAL AWAKENING

We can move from self-consciousness to God-consciousness by responding to the work of the Spirit in our life and experiencing a personal awakening. I have been a Christian for quite some time now. As the old folks used to say, "This is not my first rodeo!" I have seen many movements in the church over the years. I grew up on the tail end of what was known as the "Discipleship Movement," also known as the "Shepherding Movement." This movement focused on personal accountability and submission to authority. Although it was founded on biblical principles, it became extremely imbalanced and gave rise to severe cases of manipulation and control. I knew of instances where people were even told whom to marry, where to work, and where to send their children to school.

Because of people's hurt and brokenness, this movement gave rise to the need for inner healing, which became another movement in the church. Many people were encouraged to search deep within and go back to issues in their childhood and early adulthood and walk through these painful experiences with the help of Jesus so they could become whole.

While inner healing can be a great means of helping people, it can also become a handicap if the emphasis is wrong. I believe a better means is a radical encounter with the Holy Spirit. Nothing can take the place of a personal supernatural awakening. When we are impacted, on a personal level, with the reality of who Jesus is, our lives are profoundly transformed. This is why the church must have an understanding of who the Holy Spirit truly is and how He works in our lives. The Holy Spirit is the key to bringing the life of God "on earth as it is in heaven." He moves us from self-consciousness to God-consciousness.

THE GLOBAL AWAKENING

Just as individual believers and local churches need awakening, the global body of Christ needs awakening. As I said earlier, I believe this awakening, or reformation, has already begun. Charismatic Christianity is the fasting-growing segment in the worldwide church. Why? Because people everywhere are longing to encounter a supernatural God. For this reason, I believe that houses of awakening are emerging all over the earth, and they will fuel the global awakening of the body of Christ. There will be instances of the lame walking, the dead being raised, and creative miracles occurring. Imagine what will happen when our churches move from being "seeker friendly" to "awakening friendly"!

It all begins with the focus of your consciousness. Are you self-conscious or God-conscious? The answer to this question will determine your capacity for the miraculous. The purpose of this book is to create in you a desire for something more. The only way you will receive this "more" is if you move out of the way! That's right! Get out of the way! The apostle Peter was called to lead the church in a new era, but he first had to get over his past errors. He had failed the Lord, and he had failed himself. However, the God we serve is a God of new beginnings. At the time of the crucifixion, Peter ran from persecution and denied Jesus. But after Peter was restored by Jesus and filled with the Holy Spirit, he had the courage to face the persecution and proclaim the power of the cross. God is not looking for a generation of self-conscious or self-righteous religious people. He is looking for those who are broken and need to be restored. He is looking for those who can testify of the working of His miraculous power in their lives. Are you such a person? Now is time for you to release an awakening!

PRAYER FOR AWAKENING

Father, in the name of Jesus, I thank You for Your *mighty power*! Thank You for the spirit of revelation in the knowledge of You. Thank You for awakening me out of spiritual slumber and bringing me into the consciousness of who You are and what You have given me in Christ. I declare that the spirit of slumber is broken off of me, my family, and my community, in the name of Jesus. Lord, just as Adam and Eve walked with You in the cool of the day, I desire intimate fellowship with You. Bring me into the reality of Your supernatural presence and power daily. Cleanse my life from anything that would hinder my fellowship with You. It is my desire to please You in every area of my life. Therefore, I receive the cleansing that comes from Your Word to make me a vessel of honor, sanctified and fit for the Master's use. I declare that awakening touches everyone around me. In the name of Jesus, amen!

MIRACLE INSIGHTS

1. Is there a difference between revival and awakening? If so, what is the difference?

2. Where is the next great move of God going to come from?

3. What does the Scripture mean when it says that living water will flow out of our innermost being?

4. What is the difference between God-consciousness and self-consciousness?

SCHOOL OF THE MIRACULOUS PRACTICUM

1. Would you say you are more self-conscious or God-conscious? Why? If you tend to focus on your frailties and sin, then meditate on God's Word and worship Him consistently each day so that you can remain continually aware of God's presence and provision for you.

2. Ask God to give you a personal supernatural awakening of the reality of who Jesus is and what He has done for you, so you can experience an infilling of the Holy Spirit and healing from the hurts, discouragements, and failings of the past. Remember that God is a God of new beginnings! Ask Him to move in supernatural ways in your life so you can testify of His miraculous kingdom power and minister that power to others.

3. Have you ever received negative comments from other people for having supernatural encounters with God or walking in the miraculous? If so, how did you react? Don't be discouraged about these negative experiences, but give them to God and keep moving forward in His kingdom purposes. Allow these Bible passages to encourage you: 2 Corinthians 1:3–7 and Philippians 4:4–8.

11

EVERYDAY MIRACLES AND THE POWER OF PRAYER

"Verily, verily, I say to you, The Son can do nothing of Himself, but what He sees the Father do: for what things soever He does, these also does the Son likewise."
—John 5:19

Something good is going to happen to you today!" I often use this declaration during our church's early-morning prayer calls, in which people can phone in their prayer requests and agree in prayer for others. The reason I use this expression is that I expect miracles every day, and I desire to stir that expectation in other people's hearts. I continually live in the anticipation that something miraculous will occur. Whether I am praying for someone in the grocery store or requesting supernatural provision, I am always looking for ways in which God is working. Ultimately, the most miraculous event you and I can participate in is bringing someone to Christ.

SECRET TO THE SUPERNATURAL:

LIVING IN A CONTINUAL STATE OF EXPECTANCY

POSITIONS YOU TO EXPERIENCE THE MIRACULOUS.

Remember that the attitude of expectancy is the atmosphere for miracles. Another way of stating it is this: *expectation leads to manifestation.* The more you develop an expectation for the miraculous, the more miracles you will see. You may ask, "Can I really walk in miracles daily?" I think a better question would be, "Do I really *want* to walk in miracles daily?" If you have a spirit of expectation every single day, you will see the manifestation of that anticipation.

WATCHING AND PRAYING

How do we develop an attitude of expectancy? One major way is by prayer and intercession in harmony with God's Word. As we noted earlier, a prayer never prayed can never be answered, and a demand never placed can never be met! Consistent prayer is the catalyst for a spirit of expectancy. The more we pray according to the will of God, the more we increase our expectations. The Scriptures tell us, *"Pray without ceasing"* (1 Thessalonians 5:17). Why should we engage in continuous prayer? Prayer connects us to the spiritual realm, where miracles are born. Unfortunately, in the Western world, many believers have yet to embrace a lifestyle of prayer and intercession.

Jesus lived in a state of expectancy because He consistently communed with the Father. Would you agree that Jesus operated in the miraculous daily? If so, remember what He told us: *"Verily, I say to you, he that believes on Me, the works that I do shall he do also; and greater works than these shall he do; because I go to My Father"* (John 14:12).

Prayer is indeed the spiritual life-force of the supernatural. The Bible tells us, *"The effectual fervent prayer of a righteous man avails much"* (James 5:16). The term *"effectual fervent"* comes from the Greek word *energeo*, which means "to be active, efficient" or "to be operative, be at work, put forth power." The Greek word translated *"prayer"* in this verse means "a seeking, asking, entreating." Prayer energizes our spiritual lives and postures us to perceive the things of the Spirit. The more we pray, the more we increase our level of expectation, and the more we increase our level of expectation, the more we tap into the supernatural power of God.

THINGS THAT HINDER EXPECTANCY

Just as there are things that can fuel an attitude of expectancy, there are things that can hinder it, and in turn, hinder the miracles that God wants to manifest in our lives. One hindrance to expectancy is sin. By sin, I am referring to willful sin or iniquity. We have noted that willful sin in our life can destroy our confidence in God. While it is true that we all sin and fall short of the glory of God (see Romans 3:23), we can be intentional about removing any leaven from our lives that would compromise our faith and trust in God.

Sin is an expectancy killer! It brings guilt, shame, and condemnation. Many people are so busy battling with sin in their lives that they don't have the energy to focus on miracles. You cannot walk in condemnation and expectancy at the same time. If there is anything in your life that is causing you guilt, shame, or condemnation before the Lord, lay it down at His feet right now! Acknowledge whatever it is, repent of it, and turn back to God in faith and expectancy.

Speaking of sin, one of the most debilitating forces in the life of a believer is bitterness and resentment. When Christians refuse to forgive those who have hurt, disappointed, or wounded them (no matter the offense), they open their lives to spiritual darkness. Your faith cannot grow in the dark! It needs the light of truth and the pure water of the Word of God if it is to flourish. It is nearly impossible to be hopeful and expectant when you are bitter toward someone. Forgive! This will allow your faith to function the way it is supposed to. Jesus said,

And when you stand praying, forgive, if you have anything against any: that your Father also which is in heaven may forgive you your trespasses. —Mark 11:25

Jesus had just been speaking about faith (see verses 20–24), but then He brought up the issue of forgiveness. Why?

For in Jesus Christ neither circumcision avails any thing, nor uncircumcision; but faith which works by love.   —Galatians 5:6

Our faith works by love. Therefore, if we are offended, resentful, and bitter, we are not walking in love and our faith is not working.

RECEIVING OUR DAILY BREAD

Since prayer increases our level of expectation, what kind of prayers should we pray? In Matthew 6:9–13, Jesus provided a model of prayer for all believers to follow, which has come to be known as the Lord's Prayer. Ultimately, this prayer is about establishing the pattern of the kingdom in our lives. Here are some essential truths that this model prayer includes:

1. God is our Father.

2. His name is holy.

3. His kingdom is supreme and eminent.

4. God's will is to be done on earth as it is in heaven.

5. We are to ask for and receive our daily bread.

6. We are to pray not to be led into temptation, and to be delivered from evil.

7. We are to walk in forgiveness and release debts we hold against others.

8. The kingdom, power, and glory belong to God.

Notice that within this pattern of prayer, we are admonished to ask for and expect our daily bread:

Give us this day our daily bread.   —Matthew 6:11

This request does not just refer to physical food, but also to the miraculous power and provision of God in our lives—*every single day*. Not a day should go by that you don't expect to see the hand of God manifest in your life. Remember that when we talk about a miraculous way of life, we are talking about the daily pursuit of the presence and power of God. This is why consistency is vital in living a supernatural lifestyle. To see the demonstration of God's power, we must pray consistently. We must meditate upon God's Word consistently. We must worship God consistently.

RELEASING MIRACLES THROUGH PRAYER

"Lord, please bless this food I am about to receive."

"Help, Lord, I'm in trouble!"

Have you ever prayed these types of prayers? If you have, you are in good company. Many believers have. There is certainly nothing wrong with praying this way, but it is very important to understand that prayer is so much more than these basic requests. Again, prayer is the divine catalyst for living a supernatural life. Although we have discussed the effects of prayer in various places throughout this book, its importance cannot be overstated, and I now want to go deeper into this topic. There are millions of believers all over the world who have yet to realize the supernatural potency of prayer.

Praying always with all prayer and supplication in the Spirit, and watching thereto with all perseverance and supplication for all saints.
—Ephesians 6:18

We are admonished by the Word of God to engage in energetic and heartfelt prayer. When I first became a believer, I began praying three to six hours a day. Little did I know that this was a major key to releasing miracles. Prayer is like plugging into an electrical outlet. The stronger the connection, the greater the measure of power released.

Every time we pray, something supernatural takes place. In fact, prayer itself is a supernatural activity. On one occasion, I was speaking to a large crowd overseas, and toward the end of the message, I told the people there to lift their hands and release their faith. There was a man in the audience who suffered from blindness, and as I prayed, he was totally healed! Glory to God! As the saying goes, "Prayer changes things"!

I heard a story about healing evangelist Smith Wigglesworth that goes something like the following. A man interviewed the evangelist, asking about his prayer life and how often he prayed. Wigglesworth said, "Fifteen minutes!" The man was quite surprised by this response, thinking, "Surely a man of such great faith and power prayed longer than fifteen minutes!" Wigglesworth followed his answer by saying, "But I never go fifteen minutes without praying!" The moral of this story is that continuous prayer should be an integral part of the lifestyle of a believer.

PRAYING IN THE HOLY SPIRIT

The Scriptures are very clear that we are to pray without ceasing, and the only way we can do this is to pray in the Holy Spirit.

But you, beloved, building up yourselves on your most holy faith, praying in the Holy Ghost. —Jude 1:20

For if I pray in an unknown tongue, my spirit prays, but my understanding is unfruitful. —1 Corinthians 14:14

To pray in the Spirit means, first of all, to pray Spirit-directed prayers. Often, it means praying in a God-given language, a "tongue of men or of angels." (See 1 Corinthians 13:1.) Praying in tongues is a secret weapon in supernatural living. We usually receive the gift of praying in tongues when we are baptized in the Holy Spirit. (This kind of tongues is a heavenly gift for our personal prayer life and edification, distinct from the gifts of

SECRET TO THE SUPERNATURAL:

PRAYING IN THE HOLY SPIRIT ACTIVATES YOUR SPIRIT

AND CAUSES YOU TO BE SENSITIVE TO THE PRESENCE

AND POWER OF GOD.

tongues and interpretation that are given to be exercised in the corporate church as we gather with other believers for worship and teaching. We will talk more about spiritual gifts in the next chapter.) First Corinthians 14:14 says that when we pray in an unknown tongue, our spirit prays. Every time we pray in tongues, we build up our spirit in faith. Praying in tongues alone does not give us faith, but it strengthens and builds the faith we already possess.

I want you to grasp this truth: every time you pray, you are releasing something spiritual into the atmosphere. Every time you pray, something changes, even if it isn't immediately discernible. When I was in college, I witnessed a young man engaging in a harsh discourse with a young woman. When the man saw me, he threatened me, saying that he would hurt me. So, I refrained from engaging him. Later that day, as I was walking down the street, I saw the same young man driving by. He stopped his vehicle, got out, reached for a particular weapon, and began to walk toward me. As he came, I started to pray in the Spirit and thank God for His divine protection according to Psalm 91. As the man drew nearer to me, I continued to pray in tongues. Finally, he came within two feet of me. Suddenly, his entire countenance changed, and he began to cry and apologize. He told me that he knew who I was, and he really hadn't meant any disrespect earlier. I looked him in the eyes and told him that I forgave him and that it was okay. He turned around, walked away, got into his vehicle, and drove off. The power of prayer works!

PRAYER CHANGES YOUR PERSPECTIVE

Earlier, I quoted the saying, "Prayer changes things." While I have no doubt this statement is true, prayer chiefly changes the one doing the praying. Prayer changes *us*!

How does prayer change us? It alters our perspective. We go from having an earthbound, fallen mind-set to gaining a heavenly outlook. We have talked about the supernatural power of the transformed mind and the necessity of renewing our mind. Prayer is one of the means through which we renew our mind. Prayer cultivates the mind of Christ within us.

There was a season in my life when I fasted and prayed three days a week, every single week. During that time, God began to download supernatural keys into my spirit. I also started to have visions and supernatural revelations. I would go to the roughest communities in town, and see people saved and delivered. I didn't have one thread of fear in my body. Why? I had been spiritually supercharged through fasting and prayer.

We can train ourselves to develop a supernatural perspective about the natural circumstances in our lives. I always say that nothing catches a praying person off-guard. I encourage you to make this declaration every day as you pray:

> I have the mind of Christ. Therefore, I see the world around me from a heavenly perspective. Natural limitations are not a hindrance for me.

THE FATHER WORKS THROUGH US

Jesus said, "*Verily, verily, I say to you, The Son can do nothing of Himself, but what He sees the Father do: for what things soever He does, these also does the Son likewise.*" How did Jesus see what the Father did? Was Jesus translated to heaven every night? Here is the simple yet powerful answer to that question: no, but Jesus prayed! He prayed all the time. Through intercession, Jesus was able to gain access to the heart, mind, and will of His heavenly Father so He could carry out God's purposes on earth.

Jesus also said, "*The words that I speak to you I speak not of Myself: but the Father that dwells in Me, He does the works*" (John 14:10). This is a powerful revelation. If we are to do the works that Jesus did, we must learn how to tap into the power of prayer and allow the Father to work through us.

And this is the confidence that we have in Him, that, if we ask any thing according to His will, He hears us: and if we know that He hear us, whatsoever we ask, we know that we have the petitions that we desired of Him.   —1 John 5:14–15

What would happen if we truly realized that the Father always hears us as we pray according to His will? We probably wouldn't hesitate to pray for the sick or lead our neighbor in the prayer of salvation. We would know that the Spirit of God, living within us, is the one doing the work. He is the one producing the results! Through prayer, we partner with heaven to see the purposes of God manifested in the earth.

THE HEARING OF FAITH

He therefore that ministers to you the Spirit, and works miracles among you, does He it by the works of the law, or by the hearing of faith?   —Galatians 3:5

As we begin to walk in miracles daily, we must keep in mind that receiving miracles is not a matter of human effort but rather a byproduct of "the hearing of faith." The Bible says that *"faith comes by hearing, and hearing by the word of God"* (Romans 10:17). Faith comes as a result of our hearing the Holy Spirit speak God's Word in our inner being. Faith is our response to the revelation of God's Word for us in the now.

For example, the Word tells us, *"Now to Him that is able to do exceeding abundantly above all that we ask or think, according to the power that works in us"* (Ephesians 3:20). There is a difference between knowing this Scripture intellectually and knowing it by revelation. When the Holy Spirit speaks the Word to you, the Scripture comes alive, and you can apply what it says in practical ways. Thus, when the Word is revealed, faith comes into manifestation within us and things begin to change. Remember, we must take action to see miracles happen!

CONTEND FOR YOUR MIRACULOUS INHERITANCE

I hope you are beginning to recognize that Jesus didn't only come to bring *us into* eternal life. He came to bring eternal life *into us*. As we have seen, this refers to *zoe* life, "the God kind of life." It is the same quality of life that is in the Father. God has called us to release His life into the world every single day. Regardless of your background, education, occupation, or financial status, you have been commissioned by God to operate on a heavenly level.

Contrary to popular opinion, miracles are not random acts of God's sovereignty; instead, they are a part of our inheritance in Christ. Jesus died so that we could have a miraculous life. He paid the ultimate price for us to live supernaturally. Why would we neglect our inheritance? Have you ever thought about the miraculous in that way?

The law of supply and demand applies to many economic systems, including the economy of heaven. We must place a "demand" on heaven if we want to see the supply. We must be proactive if we want to live in the supernatural. Again, we must put a claim on all that God has promised if we want to see the manifestation of those promises.

Years ago, my wife and I decided that we were going to experience all that God had for us. Our strategy was simple yet radical: if we saw something in the Bible, we did it! We took a page out of the playbook of Mary, the mother of Jesus, who said, "Whatever He says, do it!" (See John 2:1–11.) We simply took God at His Word. Amazingly, the most interesting things began to happen—we saw results!

One time, we went around our neighborhood knocking on doors, asking people if they knew that God loved them and had an awesome plan for their lives. (This is something we learned from preacher and evangelist Dr. Rodney Howard-Browne.) Many people responded with hostility, but thankfully they couldn't tell us to leave the neighborhood because we lived there! When one particular neighbor opened the door, we asked the same question we had asked everyone else: "Do you know that God loves you and has an awesome plan for your life?" She answered, "No! I didn't know that." We were actually a bit shocked by her response. Then, she said, "Come in. I have been waiting for you guys!"

It turned out she had been going through a contentious divorce and had been ready to give up. She had said to God, "If You are real, show me You love me." Shortly after this, we arrived! We led her in the prayer of salvation, and we have discipled her and her children in the faith for the last several years. Hallelujah! Again, the greatest miracle is the miracle of salvation.

My wife and I realized that if God could use us to save people, He could also use us to heal people. So, we began ministering to the sick. People started getting healed and telling other people about their healings. Before we knew it, we were operating in miracles, and we have been doing so ever since.

What are you waiting for? Just do it! Step out in childlike faith and expectancy and watch God work.

THE DAILY DECISION TO RELEASE GOD'S POWER

The glory of this latter house shall be greater than of the former, says the LORD of hosts: and in this place will I give peace, says the LORD of hosts. —Haggai 2:9

God desires to manifest His glory in the earth, but we must make this purpose our passionate daily pursuit. God will never encroach upon the human will. He invites us into kingdom realities, but we must exercise our faith and volition in order to walk in them.

It is my sincere conviction that we are living in the last days before the return of Jesus Christ. What if I told you that you are one whom God has raised up in these last days to release miracles? What if I told you that the moment you embrace the truth that God wants to partner with you to release heaven on earth, your life will be radically catapulted into new dimensions? I invite you to make this declaration:

Today, I will hear the voice of the Holy Spirit, respond to His instruction, and release the power of God. Today, I will see miracles in my life and in the lives of those around me. I will partner with God to see the supernatural life of heaven become a reality on earth.

PRAYER FOR EXPECTATION OF THE MIRACULOUS

Father, in the name of Jesus Christ, I thank You for Your miraculous power working in me. Today, I release my expectancy for miracles, signs, and wonders. I recognize that You want to do something supernatural through my life daily. I acknowledge the power of prayer, and by faith, I access spiritual realities that go beyond the limitations of my circumstances. Father, whatever You have promised me, and whatever You have spoken concerning my life, I receive it right now. I declare that I am a vessel You have raised up in this generation to release miracles. I declare that Your Spirit catapults me into new dimensions of the supernatural presence and power of God. I am anticipating great things happening in my life because You are omnipotent and omnibenevolent. In Jesus's name, amen!

MIRACLE INSIGHTS

1. How do we develop an attitude of expectancy?

2. What are some things that can hinder our expectancy?

3. What role does prayer play in our walking in the miraculous consistently?

4. How is receiving miracles a byproduct of "the hearing of faith"?

MIRACLE TESTIMONIES

MIRACLES OF PROVISION

At one point, the Lord began to speak to my wife and me about all-night prayer. This had been a part of the culture of our church for years, but I felt like God was calling us back to that level of devotion. We began to engage in all-night prayer. During one specific season of prayer, God sent miraculous provision. Businesses began to donate things to the church. In fact, one of the top companies in our area offered thousands of dollars of services for free. Hallelujah!

In another instance, during the youth service, our nine-year-old daughter declared that she saw a vision. In this vision, during prayer, God released everything we needed for the church, but a huge spider's web held it back. Then, in this vision, she saw the web destroyed by the power of God—and the blessings were released. A week later, we got a call informing us that a brand new office suite, furniture, appliances, and equipment worth over twenty thousand dollars were being donated to us! Glory to God!

12

SPIRITUAL GIFTS AND THE MIRACULOUS

"Now concerning spiritual gifts, brethren,
I would not have you ignorant."
—1 Corinthians 12:1

As I sat at the table across from the woman, I heard a very clear word from God in my spirit: "Ask her what happened when she was six years old!" So, I reluctantly asked this complete stranger about her experience as a six-year-old girl. Tears welled up in her eyes as she narrated a painful and traumatic experience. I prayed with her and led her to Christ. Wow! I was just a young man in college, but I had experienced what the Bible calls a "word of knowledge." God supernaturally revealed something about a person's past for the purpose of leading that person to Him. This is an example of a spiritual gift. If you are going to operate in the miraculous, it is very important for you to understand the purpose and power of spiritual gifts.

SECRET TO THE SUPERNATURAL:

THE MORE INTIMATE WE ARE WITH THE HOLY SPIRIT,

THE MORE WE WILL BE ABLE TO

OPERATE IN THE GIFTS OF THE SPIRIT.

WHAT ARE SPIRITUAL GIFTS?

According to 1 Corinthians 12:1–9, spiritual gifts are special manifestations of the Holy Spirit that He distributes through and for various people and environments, for the edification of the body of Christ. In essence, spiritual gifts demonstrate to people that the Holy Spirit and the world to come are very real. First Corinthians 12 lists nine of these spiritual gifts, including:

1. Word of wisdom

2. Word of knowledge

3. Faith

4. Gifts of healing

5. Working of miracles

6. Prophecy

7. Discerning of spirits

8. Divers (various) kinds of tongues

9. Interpretation of tongues

There is nothing in Scripture that says these are the only spiritual gifts, but they are definitely the starting point. The more you learn about and understand spiritual gifts, the more you can operate in them consistently. I want to point out right away that the term "spiritual gift" is a bit misleading because it could imply this is a special endowment that only a select number of people can operate in. A better term than "gift" is probably "manifestation." After all, it is the same Holy Spirit who manifests and empowers these supernatural endowments.

Through a careful examination of the entire book of 1 Corinthians, it is clear that the church in Corinth was extremely gifted. This fact should remind us that we can be extremely gifted yet still have issues with our character. Nonetheless, Paul encourages the church to grow in their gifting. Before they can do that, they must understand the origin and function of the gifts. What is the purpose of the gifts of the Spirit? How do they operate? Paul wrote,

Now concerning spiritual gifts, brethren, I would not have you ignorant. You know that you were Gentiles, carried away to these dumb idols, even as you were led. Wherefore I give you to understand, that no man speaking by the Spirit of God calls Jesus accursed: and that no man can say that Jesus is the Lord, but by the Holy Ghost.

—1 Corinthians 12:1–3

In *The Amplified Bible*, this passage reads,

Now about the spiritual gifts [the special endowments given by the Holy Spirit], brothers and sisters, I do not want you to be uninformed. You know that when you were pagans, you were led off after speechless idols; however you were led off [whether by impulse or habit]. Therefore I want you to know that no one speaking by the [power and influence of the] Spirit of God can say, "Jesus be cursed," and no one can say, "Jesus is [my] Lord," except by [the power and influence of] the Holy Spirit.

Paul first wanted to establish that the gifts of the Spirit were from the Holy Spirit alone and were not in any way associated with the idolatry the Corinthians were accustomed to in the past. He also wanted to establish the unity of the Spirit in the gifting. "*Now there are diversities of gifts, but the same Spirit*" (1 Corinthians 12:4). Another important point is the fact that the word "*gifts*," which follows "*spiritual*" in 1 Corinthians 12:1, is in italics in the King James Version, which means that it was inserted by the translators. In the original Greek, this word does not appear. The Greek literally reads, "Now concerning spiritualities..." or "Now concerning the spiritual things...." Why is that significant? Just as the Holy Spirit bears fruit of various attributes in the lives of born-again believers (see Galatians 5:22–23), He also expresses different endowments or manifestations in the church. It is the same Spirit manifesting in diverse ways for the collective benefit of the body of Christ.

GOD'S SUPERNATURAL SYMPHONY

Some argue that the gifts of the Spirit are not in operation today, but spiritual gifts are just as relevant now as they were in the first-century church. First Corinthians 12:7 tells us plainly, *"But the manifestation of the Spirit is given to every man to profit withal."* Again, the Holy Spirit manifests various supernatural endowments in order to bring the church together and create a beautiful symphony, with the different gifts working in concert for the benefit of the entire church.

Let's review the nine gifts that Paul lists in 1 Corinthians 12: word of wisdom, word of knowledge, faith, healing, working of miracles, prophecy, discerning of spirits, various kinds of tongues, and the interpretation of tongues. The special endowments of faith, healing, and miracles are called "power gifts." They are action-oriented. But Paul encourages the church to appreciate the way the Holy Spirit manifests through each believer, and never to be jealous or prideful based upon a particular gifting.

For the body is not one member, but many. If the foot shall say, Because I am not the hand, I am not of the body; is it therefore not of the body? And if the ear shall say, Because I am not the eye, I am not of the body; is it therefore not of the body? If the whole body were an eye, where were the hearing? If the whole were hearing, where were the smelling? But now has God set the members every one of them in the body, as it has pleased Him. And if they were all one member, where were the body? But now are they many members, yet but one body.

—1 Corinthians 12:14–20

SECRET TO THE SUPERNATURAL:

ALWAYS SEEK THE GIVER,

AND YOU WILL ALWAYS FIND THE GIFT.

We can see how the theme of honoring the body of Christ is reiterated. In His sovereignty, God has placed the gifts in the church *"as He will"* (1 Corinthians 12:11), or as it pleases Him. As a result, Paul tells us, we ought to honor the gifts within the church and the people to whom those gifts have been given. Every member is important, and every member deserves to be honored and appreciated. We honor the body by recognizing and honoring the gifts of the Spirit.

Just as the church was divided over gifting in the first century, many people are divided over the gifts of the Spirit in the modern church. We have separated whole denominations based upon disagreements about speaking in tongues, healing, and prophecy. The central theme of Paul's address was to enlighten the Corinthians concerning the fact that we are all one body and each member plays a vital role in the edification of the church. Without feet, we cannot walk, and without eyes, we cannot see. Each member and function is necessary for the overall profit of the body of Christ. You would think that after two thousand years, we would have learned that lesson!

THE UNCTION TO FUNCTION

The Holy Spirit is the most important Person on earth, and one of His roles as our Helper is to endow us with supernatural function. We have been empowered by the Spirit of God to be witnesses of the resurrection of Jesus Christ. One of the ways in which we do this is through the exercise of spiritual gifts. Let's now examine each of the nine gifts or manifestations in 1 Corinthians 12 to gain a fuller understanding of how to operate in them.

WORD OF WISDOM

The word of wisdom is a supernatural revelation of the present or future. This gift is designed to instruct, exhort, and console the body of Christ. For example, a woman walked into my church whom I had never met before. When it was time for the altar call, she came to receive prayer. As she stood there, the Lord revealed to me that she was in transition and praying about her career. She needed wisdom on the right decision to make in the coming months. This was a word of wisdom, revealed to me through divine agency, that addressed a specific question of her heart. It was not based upon any natural information available to me at the time. I didn't know her, and I didn't go through her Facebook page before I released a word to her! All the information came directly from God for the purpose of encouraging and building her up.

WORD OF KNOWLEDGE

What is a word of knowledge? The Greek term for *"word"* here (as well as in *"word of wisdom"*) is *logos*, which refers to "something said (including the thought)." The Greek word translated *"knowledge"* comes from the root *ginōskō*, among whose meanings is "to know," "to understand," "to perceive," and "to feel." Often, a word of knowledge is actually a feeling or an impression given to someone by the Holy Spirit. But what really makes it a word of knowledge is when it is spoken. If the impression God gives us remains in the realm of the Spirit, it can have no benefit in the natural realm.

Remember, the purpose of a word of knowledge is to benefit the hearer, not to gratify the speaker. However, there is great satisfaction and gratification in releasing an accurate word of knowledge. I was once a keynote speaker at a workshop in Europe, and I wrote down several words and numbers that God had given to me concerning various people attending the workshop. Then, I called out a series of numbers in order. One young lady in the front row began to look distressed. Her eyes bulged out of her head, and she reluctantly raised her hand and said, "Sir, that is the PIN number to my private bank account in Nigeria!" As she continued speaking, God gave me a word for her. He revealed to me that He was going to manifest a financial breakthrough in her life. She began to weep as she told me that she had been in the country illegally because she couldn't afford the necessary papers, and she had spent her last dime coming to the workshop, believing that God would speak to her and give her a miracle! Hallelujah!

In another illustration of a word of knowledge, in November 2015, I accompanied Sid Roth on his Israel tour, and I was asked to speak at a large theater in Caesarea. The presence of God was so strong that you could feel it in the atmosphere. We began to worship God, and the glory came down. While we were in the glory realm, I spoke out that someone's eyes were being healed. There was a man in the audience who'd had double vision for as long as he could remember. When he caught the word of the Lord, he was instantly healed, and he has maintained his healing from that day.

Let me share one more example. We received a written testimony from a woman who was watching when I was a guest on Sid Roth's program *It's Supernatural!* Her son had left home, saying that he would never return. On that program, the Lord gave me a word of knowledge about a prodigal son returning. I looked into the camera and said, "He is about to come home." This woman testified that the power of God hit her. She began praying for her son, declaring that he would come home. Within seventy-two hours, the son came home, repented to his mother, and surrendered his life to God. Hallelujah!

FAITH

One of my favorite Scriptures is Hebrews 11:1: *"Now faith is the substance of things hoped for, the evidence of things not seen."* The Greek word translated *"faith"* is *pistis*, which means "conviction" or "confidence." It is the complete assurance of the truth of something. Another way to describe it is "trust." Every believer has this kind of faith because God gives it to us. (See Romans 12:3.) As we noted earlier, without this faith, we couldn't believe the gospel and be born again. However, this is not the kind of faith referred to in 1 Corinthians 12. Although the same Greek word is used, the context is very different. The gift of faith is a special endowment of the Holy Spirit to believe God for a specific manifestation or outcome.

The gift of faith often accompanies the gift of miracles. Have you noticed that some people have a "ridiculous" faith for healing or the provision of finances? They can pray for cancer patients without ever doubting that they will be healed, or they can believe, without blinking, that God will supply millions of dollars for a building project. This is the gift of faith. I personally operate in this gift of the Spirit.

GIFTS OF HEALING

The fourth gift mentioned in 1 Corinthians 12 is *"gifts of healing."* It is interesting that the King James Version uses the plural form—gifts—because there are varying gifts of healing. I vividly remember the first date my wife and I went on. At that time in her life, she suffered greatly from migraine headaches. As we were sitting and talking, I noticed that she was in pain. I asked what was wrong, and when she divulged her struggle with headaches, I immediately rebuked the migraine in the name of Jesus! To her surprise, the headache disappeared. It was miraculous!

Gifts of healing are supernatural manifestations of God's healing power through the Holy Spirit. They often manifest independent of the faith of the person receiving the healing or miracle. In other words, when gifts of healing are in manifestation, people don't necessarily have to undergo the process of developing their faith and standing on God's Word for healing. Different types of healings may manifest through different people at different times. Sometimes, people will have an anointing for healing regarding a certain part of the body or disease. For example, certain believers see miraculous results when they pray for people's eyes, while others see tremendous results in the area of cancer. It is important to develop a sensitivity to the Holy Spirit to properly understand what He desires to do at any given moment.

WORKING OF MIRACLES

He therefore that ministereth to you the Spirit, and worketh miracles among you, doeth he it by the works of the law, or by the hearing of faith? —Galatians 3:5 KJV

As we have discussed in previous chapters, miracles are part of God's plan to expand His kingdom in the earth. In the above verse, the apostle Paul asked a profound question: do those who minister the Spirit and work miracles do it by the works of the law or by the hearing of faith? Although this verse is not specifically about spiritual gifts, it gives us a profound insight into how the gifts of the Spirit operate. Miracles are the result of *"the hearing of faith."* Once, a woman was healed of terminal cancer just by listening to one of my messages online. God had revealed the illness to me, and I had called it out by name. Glory to God!

Gifts of miracles are the manifestation of the *dunamis* power of God, through the invasion of eternity into time. Miracles disrupt the natural course of events. Because they override natural processes, miracles are typically instantaneous. Miracle gifts are usually released when there is an impossible situation or circumstance. Remember how Jesus took five loaves of bread and two fish and made it into a feast fit for kings that fed more than five thousand hungry people? In the natural realm, this would have been impossible, but natural laws no longer had "legal" jurisdiction when the miracle of multiplication manifested.

PROPHECY

Follow after charity [love], and desire spiritual gifts, but rather that you may prophesy. For he that speaks in an unknown tongue speaks not to men, but to God: for no man understands him; however in the spirit he speaks mysteries. But he that prophesies speaks to men to edification, and exhortation, and comfort.   —1 Corinthians 14:1–3

One of my favorite gifts of the Spirit is prophecy. According to the above passage, it is one of God's favorite spiritual gifts as well. Paul later wrote, *"Even so you, forasmuch as you are zealous of spiritual gifts, seek that you may excel to the edifying of the church"* (1 Corinthians 14:12). Why is prophecy so important to God? I'm glad you asked! The simple gift of prophecy is for *"edification, and exhortation, and comfort."*

The Greek word translated *"prophesy"* in 1 Corinthians 14 is *prophēteuō*, which means to utter under divine inspiration. It consists of both foretelling (future events) and forth-telling (declaring the mind and counsel of

SECRET TO THE SUPERNATURAL:

ASK GOD TO OPEN YOUR SPIRITUAL EYES

SO THAT YOU CAN SEE AND DISCERN

THE SPIRITUAL WORLD AROUND YOU.

God over a person or situation). If you speak in an unknown tongue, you edify only yourself (unless there is an accompanying interpretation), but if you release a prophetic word, you edify the church. The gift of prophecy reveals the mind of God, and the church is admonished as a result of the word of the Lord.

This is why the apostle Paul said that, in the church, he would rather prophesy than speak in tongues. It doesn't mean that we should not value speaking in tongues; rather, it means that we must recognize the usefulness of prophecy in relation to the local church.

DISCERNING OF SPIRITS

Beloved, believe not every spirit, but try the spirits whether they are of God: because many false prophets are gone out into the world.
—1 John 4:1

We know that the spiritual realm is a deeper reality than the natural realm, and we need to learn to function in it. Moreover, there are two opposing kingdoms in operation in the spiritual realm: the kingdom of light and the kingdom of darkness. This is why the gift of discerning of spirits is so critical for the church as it functions in the miraculous power of God.

The Greek word for *"discerning"* is *diakrisis*, which means "a distinguishing, discerning, judging." Discernment often requires the ability to distinguish between two (sometimes similar-seeming) things. Here are some basic life examples: children must learn to discern the difference between a hot stovetop and a cold stovetop, and human beings have to learn to distinguish between right and wrong. In the spiritual world, discerning of spirits is the supernatural ability to recognize and differentiate between spirits. Notice that I said "spirits" and not "people." This gift is not a license for judging or condemning someone else. There is no such thing as the gift of suspicion!

Discerning of spirits enables a believer to recognize or sense the presence of angels, demons, the Holy Spirit, and human spirits. Once, when I was experiencing a very difficult season in my life and ministry, I felt as if I was going through depression. One day, I mustered the courage to pray, even though I didn't feel like it. As I struggled in prayer, I had an impression that an angel was in my room. This angel took an ice-cold bucket of water and poured it on top of my head. Immediately, I jumped up and began praising God with a newfound joy! After this powerful experience, I inquired of the Lord concerning the name of that angel. He told me, "That angel is Joy." Now, I experience angelic visitations often. In fact, an angel of breakthrough travels with me on all of my international trips.

Wow! The truth is that there are angels (and demons) all around, but you must allow the Holy Spirit to impart to you the ability to recognize them. The gift of discerning of spirits is not some cute or random gift that exists for the purpose of entertaining believers. Instead, it is for intercession and deliverance. This gift helps us to partner with heaven's agenda to see miracles on the earth. It also helps us to pray and exercise spiritual authority over demonic powers. God desires to unveil our spiritual eyes and allow us to see matters in the invisible realm. Those whom He has gifted heavily in the prophetic will often operate in discerning of spirits as well.

DIVERS, OR VARIOUS, KINDS OF TONGUES

In the law it is written, With men of other tongues and other lips will I speak to this people; and yet for all that will they not hear Me, says the Lord. —1 Corinthians 14:21

On the day of Pentecost, the Holy Spirit filled the upper room where one hundred and twenty disciples of Jesus were gathered. Cloven tongues of fire sat on the each of these disciples, and they spoke with other tongues as the Spirit gave them utterance. (See Acts 2.) This was the first time any follower of Jesus had spoken in other tongues. It was a sign of the outpouring of the Holy Spirit as prophesied in Joel 2.

In Acts 10, in the account of the centurion Cornelius, we see another manifestation of tongues, which demonstrated that Cornelius and those gathered with him had received the Holy Spirit. However, when Paul addressed the gift of various kinds of tongues, he was not referring to the initial evidence of the baptism of the Holy Spirit, as was the case in this incident, but rather to a special endowment from the Holy Spirit that allows people to speak in various tongues or languages, especially as a public discourse in the church.

I once knew a man who had ministered in India. He told me that he didn't know the native language, but as he was preaching, he began to speak in a tongue unknown to him. While he couldn't understand what he was saying, the local people could understand every word. This has happened many times. The gift of various kinds of tongues can also refer to a situation in which a person becomes supernaturally fluent in heavenly languages. There is supernatural power connected to speaking in *"divers kinds of tongues,"* and it is typically accompanied by a miraculous manifestation.

INTERPRETATION OF TONGUES

I would that you all spoke with tongues, but rather that you prophesied: for greater is he that prophesies than he that speaks with tongues, except he interpret, that the church may receive edifying.
—1 Corinthians 14:5

In 1 Corinthians 14, Paul was addressing a specific challenge in the church: people were operating in too many gifts at the same time, and it was a recipe for confusion and disaster. To illustrate the problem, Paul told the Corinthians, in effect, that if everyone were to begin speaking in unknown tongues at the top of their lungs, then a person visiting the church for the

SECRET TO THE SUPERNATURAL:

IF YOU WILL LEARN TO SPEAK HEAVEN'S LANGUAGE,

YOU WILL BEGIN TO SEE HEAVEN'S RESULTS.

first time would think the people there were insane. Why? Because they would not be speaking intelligible words. (See 1 Corinthians 14:23.)

The gift of interpretation of tongues was very valuable in the first-century church, and it is equally valuable today. After a public discourse in an unknown tongue, the gift of interpretation—the translation of the message into intelligible speech that edifies the people present—is much needed and powerful. I grew up in a church where a message in tongues was given every Sunday morning, and believers who operated in the gift of interpretation would speak out the prophetic message in English so that the church could be encouraged and built up.

PRAYER FOR SPIRITUAL GIFTS

Father, in the name of Jesus, I thank You for who You are and all that You have done in my life. I recognize that You are the giver of good gifts, and all that is good and perfect comes from You. Therefore, I receive the gifts of the Spirit into my life. Through the Holy Spirit, I am empowered to operate in the supernatural. I thank You that the manifestation of Your Holy Spirit abounds in and through my life, enabling me to impact my world for the glory of God. Through the gifts of the Spirit, I tap into and release Your miraculous power. As You instruct us in 1 Corinthians 12:31, I earnestly pursue the best gifts so that I may be instrumental in edifying the body of Christ. In Matthew 7:7, Your Word says, *"Ask, and it shall be given you; seek, and you shall find; knock, and it shall be opened to you."* Therefore, I ask for all the gifts that I am able to receive and walk in. I pray this in the name of Jesus, amen!

MIRACLE INSIGHTS

1. What does the Bible mean by the term "spiritual gifts"?

2. What are the nine gifts of the Spirit listed in 1 Corinthians 12?

3. What did Paul say is the most important spiritual gift in the church?

4. What is the relationship between spiritual gifts and operating in the miraculous?

SCHOOL OF THE MIRACULOUS PRACTICUM

1. Which spiritual gift (or gifts) has God given you? How are you using it? How can you increase your use of this gift to build up others in the church and minister to those who do not yet know God? Seek God for other gifts He desires to give you, and begin to walk in them.

2. If you don't know which spiritual gift you have been given, ask God to reveal it to you by His Holy Spirit, the Gift Giver, and to help you grow in this gift as you continue to mature in Christlike character.

3. How is your particular gift necessary for the edification of the church? How can you better appreciate and honor the diverse gifts within the church and the individuals to whom they have been given? Make a point to express your appreciation to two people this week for exercising their gifts of the Spirit as the Lord leads them.

13

THE SUPERNATURAL CHURCH

"And I say also to you, That you are Peter, and upon this rock I will build My church; and the gates of hell shall not prevail against it."
—Matthew 16:18

What is the church? Is it a building with a steeple on top? Is it a large cathedral? Is it place where people drink coffee, wear skinny jeans, and play contemporary Christian music? While these various expressions of faith are fine in themselves, they really have nothing to do with the definition of the church—either the worldwide body of Christ or the local body of believers.

The fact is, the average Christian doesn't really know what the church is. Before we talk about the meaning of the church and how essential it is for living a supernatural lifestyle, I think it would be beneficial to remind ourselves of what the church is *not*:

+ The church is not a building.
+ The church is not an organization.

SECRET TO THE SUPERNATURAL:

NEVER UNDERESTIMATE THE POWER OF UNITY IN

RELEASING THE ANOINTING.

- The church is not a particular denomination.

- The church is not the invention of human beings.

Now that we know what the church is not, let's look at what the church actually is:

- The church is the body of Christ. (See Ephesians 1:22–23; Colossians 1:24.)

- The church is a spiritual organism; it is alive. (See 1 Peter 2:4–8.)

- The church is the full number of believers (on earth and in heaven), as well as the local gathering of believers, transcending denominationalism. (See, for example, Ephesians 2:13–22.)

- The church is the supernatural institution of God.

A SUPERNATURAL COMMUNITY

Let's explore this last point. The church of the Lord Jesus Christ is a supernatural entity. When you remove the supernatural power of God from the church, you don't have the church anymore; you merely have a religious organization. This means that if you are a member of the church of Jesus Christ, then you are a member of a supernatural community. Wow!

In Matthew 16:18, the verse quoted at the beginning of this chapter, remember that the Greek word translated *"church,"* *ekklesia*, comes from a political term, one of whose meanings is "an assembly of the people convened at the public place of the council for the purpose of deliberating." It is derived from the compound words *ek* and *kaleo*, which literally mean "called out." These Greek words represent "the gathering of called-out ones." The church worldwide, or universal, is the collective gathering of God's people. We, the church, have been "called out" of the world to convene on behalf of the kingdom of God. The apostle Peter puts it this way:

But you are a chosen generation, a royal priesthood, a holy nation, a peculiar people; that you should show forth the praises of Him who has called you out of darkness into His marvelous light. —1 Peter 2:9

SECRET TO THE SUPERNATURAL:

THE CHURCH IS BUILT ON THE REVELATION

OF JESUS CHRIST. EVERY TIME WE GATHER

TOGETHER IN HIS NAME, THE ANOINTING FOR MIRACLES,

SIGNS, AND WONDERS IS RELEASED.

A COLLECTIVE ANOINTING

The Scriptures declare that when God's people gather together in unity, the anointing flows.

Behold, how good and how pleasant it is for brethren to dwell together in unity! It is like the precious ointment upon the head, that ran down upon the beard, even Aaron's beard: that went down to the skirts of his garments. —Psalm 133:1–2

This anointing is what I referred to in an earlier chapter as the "dynamic, yoke-destroying, burden-removing, supernatural power of God." When the church embraces her true identity, we will see signs, wonders, and miracles. When is the last time you tapped into the collective anointing of the church? This is God's plan for us!

And when [Jesus's followers] had prayed, the place was shaken where they were assembled together; and they were all filled with the Holy Ghost, and they spoke the word of God with boldness. And the multitude of them that believed were of one heart and of one soul: neither said any of them that any of the things which he possessed was his own; but they had all things common. And with great power gave the apostles witness of the resurrection of the Lord Jesus: and great grace was upon them all. —Acts 4:31–33

The church was God's idea, not man's. Jesus Himself is the one who identified and established the church, and He continues to build it to this day. The Lord said, "*I will build My church; and the gates of hell shall not prevail against it.*"

WE ARE THE CHURCH!

Some Christians don't place a priority on attending a local church. They may think they can serve God on their own, believing that their

SECRET TO THE SUPERNATURAL:

THE CHURCH IS A SUPERNATURAL ORGANISM,

BUILT ON A SUPERNATURAL FOUNDATION,

MEANT TO RELEASE SUPERNATURAL POWER.

THE FOUNDATION DETERMINES THE POTENTIAL.

faith is solely an individual matter between themselves and God. Or, they may feel that their past sins keep them from entering into fellowship with other believers, even though God has promised forgiveness to those who come to Him in repentance. But if they really knew what the church was, they would eagerly meet regularly with other believers for worship, prayer, teaching, and ministry. They would recognize the power of the blessed community!

There are other Christians who have a misconception about the nature of the body of Christ. I often hear people say, "I am the church!" That is a very disturbing line of thought; it is erroneous and a misunderstanding of Scripture. It is not, "I am the church," but "*We* are the church"!

To borrow from the apostle Paul's analogy in 1 Corinthians 12:14–27, can you imagine your hand saying, "I am the body"? How ridiculous would that be? We know that the hand is not the body; rather, it is *a part of* the body. The same concept is true spiritually. All believers—collectively—are the church. And together, we are anointed to advance into the territory of the enemy and liberate the regions of captivity that have been occupied by demonic powers, so that the culture of heaven can be established in those places.

THE HEAVENLY PATTERN

When the Israelites lived in the wilderness after their deliverance from Egypt, God instructed Moses on how to build the tabernacle, the place where the Lord would dwell with His people. This tabernacle—and later the temple in Jerusalem, which replaced it—and all its furnishings, were to be constructed according to their pattern in heaven.

And look that you make them after their pattern, which was showed you in the mount.					—Exodus 25:40

Who serve to the example and shadow of heavenly things, as Moses was admonished of God when he was about to make the tabernacle: for,

See, says He, that you make all things according to the pattern showed
to you in the mount.   —Hebrews 8:5

Today, the church and individual believers are the temple of God, because His Spirit dwells in us. (See, for example, 1 Corinthians 6:19.)

Moses was a type of Christ. God raised him to be a deliverer, to liberate God's people from bondage to the oppressive system of Egypt and bring them into the promised land. Jesus Christ is our Deliverer, who has liberated us from slavery to sin and brought us into His promised kingdom.

[God] has delivered us from the power of darkness, and has translated
us into the kingdom of His dear Son.   —Colossians 1:13

Christ not only delivered us from sin, but He also built the church according to the heavenly pattern. That is why He included this phrase in His model prayer: *"Your kingdom come, Your will be done in earth, as it is in heaven"* (Matthew 6:10). This is what I believe is the heavenly pattern for the calling and work of the church:

1. Preach the kingdom. (See, for example, Matthew 10:7; 24:14.)

2. Demonstrate the power of God. (See, for example, Mark 16:17–18, 20; Luke 9:2.)

3. Call people to repentance. (See, for example, Luke 24:46–47.)

4. Make disciples. (See Matthew 28:18–20.)

5. Continue in prayer, the Word, and fellowship. (See Acts 2:42.)

6. Walk in love. (See, for example, Ephesians 5:2; 2 John 1:5–6.)

7. Repeat steps 1–6.

Is the modern-day church following this heavenly pattern? Some people say that the church needs to adapt what it stands for to the new age in which we are living, and that it needs new strategies. While we can certainly use all of the modern technologies available to us to spread the gospel, the church doesn't need to "modernize" the Word of God or develop radically new strategies. I believe we need to go back to the heavenly pattern. When the church reflects the glory and power of heaven, then hell can't hinder its progress, and we can fulfill what God has called us to do.

Our churches must become houses of prayer for all nations. (See, for example, Matthew 21:13.) We must see the gospel preached; people saved, healed, and delivered; and the dead raised to life. Are these far-fetched ideas? Fantastic dreams? No! They come from the Word of God. People in the world need to see the power of God demonstrated in a real and tangible way.

I declare that the church is rising in power and glory! A remnant of God's people is being stirred in the earth today! Believers will not cower in the face of fear. They will not be intimidated by the enemy. They will not allow hurt, disappointment, or the shame of the past to keep them from becoming a part of a local assembly of Christians. Instead, they will boldly proclaim that their lives have been established upon the revelation of Jesus Christ.

WE HAVE THE KEYS OF THE KINGDOM

Jesus gave the church the keys of the kingdom of heaven:

I say also to you, That you are Peter, and upon this rock I will build My church; and the gates of hell shall not prevail against it. And I will give to you the keys of the kingdom of heaven: and whatsoever you shall bind on earth shall be bound in heaven: and whatsoever you shall loose on earth shall be loosed in heaven. —Matthew 16:18–19

The Greek word translated "keys" is *kleis*, which is used "metaphorically in the New Testament to denote power and authority of various kinds." It indicates that "the keeper of the keys has the power to open and

SECRET TO THE SUPERNATURAL:

GOD'S WAY OF DOING THINGS IS AGELESS AND

EVERLASTING; IT ALWAYS WORKS!

to shut." Just as certain natural keys can unlock and lock doors, Jesus has given the church spiritual keys to unlock and lock situations in the earth.

In the book of Acts, we see much evidence of a supernatural church that demonstrated God's power before the people. There was so much glory and love in the church that people released their goods and brought their wealth into the church for the benefit of those in need, so that no one lacked anything. (See Acts 4:34–35.) This is one of the reasons why it is so important for the church to embrace its supernatural identity. There are certain heavenly blessings and provisions that will not be released in the earthly realm until we utilize the supernatural keys that Christ has given us. Miracles are one of the keys of the kingdom. Miracles authenticate the message of the cross, demonstrate the power of God, and draw people to the King and His kingdom.

Today, the manifestation of the supernatural in the church is overdue! There is a family member who is waiting for you to embrace the full message of the kingdom and show them how real God is. There is a fellow employee waiting for you to demonstrate the power and love of Jesus in your job and in your personal life. Even now, there may be someone who is contemplating suicide, and they need to see the miraculous power of God that is available to set them free from their bondage.

I believe that the church will be taken seriously when we accept and walk in the mandate Jesus gave us nearly two thousand years ago:

Go you therefore, and teach ["make disciples of" NIV] all nations, baptizing them in the name of the Father, and of the Son, and of the Holy Ghost: teaching them to observe all things whatsoever I have commanded you. —Matthew 28:19–20

We are to go into all the world and make disciples, teaching them to obey what Jesus has commanded. We have been commissioned by God to teach His supernatural ways to all nations.

WE ARE THE LIGHT OF THE WORLD

When I was growing up, we often had power outages at our home. (Some of these outages were the result of Mother Nature, while others were the result of Father Power Company, who came to shut off the electricity when the bill wasn't paid!) For this reason, my family always had spare matches, oil and kerosene lamps, and flashlights on hand to give light in the darkness.

Jesus told us that as we reflect His light, we will be the light of the world. Light seems to shine even brighter in the darkness.

I am the light of the world: he that follows Me shall not walk in darkness, but shall have the light of life. —John 8:12

You are the light of the world. A city that is set on a hill cannot be hidden. Neither do men light a candle, and put it under a bushel, but on a candlestick; and it gives light to all that are in the house. Let your light so shine before men, that they may see your good works, and glorify your Father which is in heaven. —Matthew 5:14–16

In biblical days, people didn't have fluorescent or LED technology, so they had to depend on fire to provide light. If we are going to be the light of the world, we must be on fire for God! "*Neither do men light a candle, and put it under a bushel, but on a candlestick; and it gives light to all that are in the house.*"

The Greek word translated *"light"* in the phrase *"gives light"* is *lampo*, which means "to shine," "to beam," or "to radiate brilliancy." Whether a lamp consists of an electric bulb with a metal holder and fabric shade, or burns gas or a liquid fuel and consists of a wick or mantle and a glass shade, it is a device for providing light.

A lamp does not operate on its own. It must be activated by human agencies. Additionally, it does not produce light in itself, but rather harnesses it. Why is this analogy important? Jesus is the Light, but we must yield ourselves to Him in order to release His light to the people around us. We are lamps in our generation. We must "wick" the oil of the Holy Spirit in order to fuel the fire of awakening, which will illuminate the darkness in our society.

A lamp is also a symbol of revelation. The church is responsible for illuminating people with the knowledge of God, becoming His instruments to fill the earth with His glory. (See, for example, Isaiah 11:9; Habakkuk 2:14.)

In [Jesus] was life; and the life was the light of men.... There was a man sent from God, whose name was John. The same came for a witness, to bear witness of the Light, that all men through Him might believe. He was not that Light, but was sent to bear witness of that Light. That was the true Light, which lights every man that comes into the world. —John 1:4, 6–9

PRAYER FOR THE SUPERNATURAL CHURCH

Father, in the name of Jesus, I thank You for who You are and all that You have done and continue to do in my life. In Your Word, the Lord Jesus declared that He will build His church, and the gates of hell will not prevail against it. Thank You for empowering Your people to be the *ekklesia* that You have called us to be. Thank You that we carry the legislative authority of the kingdom of God on earth. You are raising a generation of sons and daughters who operate in Your supernatural presence, power, and love—this is Your definition of a supernatural church. I declare that my church is a supernatural church and that we operate according to the heavenly pattern. Your kingdom is a kingdom of power; therefore, I declare that miracles, signs, and wonders are our portion. I walk in and release Your supernatural power daily. I declare that miracles are a natural part of my life and the lives of the people around me. Thank You for releasing Your anointing to destroy shackles of shame, guilt, condemnation, and fear. In the name of Jesus, amen!

MIRACLE INSIGHTS

1. What does a supernatural church look like? What examples of a supernatural church do we see in Scripture?

2. What is the "collective anointing"? How do we tap into this anointing?v

3. Name the seven aspects of the heavenly pattern for the calling and work of the church. Does your church follow this pattern?

4. The Bible says that we are *"the light of the world."* What does this mean?

MIRACLE TESTIMONIES

MIRACLES OF HEALING

A little boy who came to our church couldn't speak, even though he was three years old. We prayed over him and declared that he would operate normally. After we prayed, he began to speak and function age-appropriately. We have seen a number of children on the spectrum be healed and begin to function normally, no matter what disorder they have been diagnosed with.

———

One person who attended a healing summit reported, "On April 26, 2018, I was at a weekend healing summit with Pastor Kynan and was healed of chronic migraine syndrome after nineteen years. Pastor also prophesied over me that another round of financial blessings would come into my life. In May 2018, my son got full-time work to help with our finances. *Amen* and *glory to God.*"

14

FIVE KEYS TO ACTIVATING GOD'S POWER

"Then he answered and spoke to me, saying, This is the word of the
LORD to Zerubbabel, saying, Not by might, nor by power, but by My
Spirit, says the LORD of hosts."
—Zechariah 4:6

In this final chapter, I want to give you five keys to activating God's power in your life: (1) submit, (2) obey, (3) expect, (4) stand, and (5) respond.

1. SUBMIT

To submit means to lay aside your own agenda so you can listen and respond to God's agenda. He may take you in an entirely different direction than you originally planned to go. His direction often leads us in remarkable ways and leaves us awestruck!

One time, I noticed that a close friend was struggling to hear God's voice, causing them great frustration. However, I also observed that during corporate prayer times, my friend would try to direct their prayers according to premeditated agendas, and also to direct the prayers of others, telling everyone how to pray and what to pray. This close friend is a wonderful Christian, but they were not leaving room for the Holy Spirit to direct them or others who were praying. When we do this, the Holy Spirit is blocked from giving us the words to pray or prophetic insights for ourselves and others. We need to give the Holy Spirit room to speak to us.

2. OBEY

Second, do all that God instructs you to do in His Word and by the leading of His Spirit. It is important to respond to God's precious directions and invitations in a timely manner. Obedience to the Lord includes following established biblical patterns and divine principles. For example, signs and wonders are meant primarily to bear witness to the power of the gospel: *"God also bearing them witness, both with signs and wonders, and with divers miracles, and gifts of the Holy Ghost, according to His own will"* (Hebrews 2:4). Consequently, as we preach the gospel, we need to put in a claim, or demand, on God's power to bring signs and wonders as confirmation of the message.

But be you doers of the word, and not hearers only, deceiving your own selves.
—James 1:22

---

3. EXPECT

Living in expectation that God will work signs, wonders, and miracles is like playing catch with your hands open, your eyes focused, your knees bent, and your body leaning forward, ready to receive the ball. If you close your hands like a fist, turn and face the opposite way, become distracted by conversation, or give up and sit down, you will miss the ball. God is continuously releasing answers and manifestations and offering life-changing encounters, so don't miss out! Stay ready!

As we remain prepared, we also need to learn to pray more specifically.

Verily I say to you, Whatsoever you shall bind on earth shall be bound in heaven: and whatsoever you shall loose on earth shall be loosed in heaven. Again I say to you, That if two of you shall agree on earth as touching any thing that they shall ask, it shall be done for them of My Father which is in heaven. —Matthew 18:18–19

One day, I was praying with my children, and we didn't pray for any one particular thing. We prayed a general prayer for everything and everyone. We prayed for whatever came to mind, that our day would go well, and for the healing of some minor conditions we were dealing with. Then, when we listened for the Holy Spirit to speak, we didn't hear anything. The Holy Spirit later instructed me that in order to receive answers, we must (1) be in total agreement with our fellow intercessors, (2) pray fervently, and (3) take time to wait on the Lord, asking, "Lord, speak to me." That is how we remain in expectation and receive breakthroughs during our prayer times.

4. STAND

The fourth key is to stand firmly on the Word of God. When our faith is based on His Word, we can have confidence that He will intervene. There is nothing like knowing "I am in God's perfect will." The Bible says, *"And this is the confidence that we have in Him, that, if we ask any thing according to His will, He hears us: and if we know that He hear us, whatsoever we ask, we know that we have the petitions that we desired of Him"* (1 John 5:14–15). When you are in God's will, "you know that you know" that you will see His manifestations.

5. RESPOND

Fifth, as you engage in heartfelt prayer based on God's Word, the Holy Spirit will give you revelation and emphasize specific promises from the Scriptures. God will send people to you, either to help you in some way or to be ministered to. He will highlight a word from your pastor or another preacher. The Holy Spirit will even speak to you in the middle of the day with instruction, caution, direction, and advice. You have to believe, receive, and take action on the words He gives. Sometimes, they may be a direct instruction, a call to trust Him and release your faith, or the guidance to wait. Other times, they may be a guideline for your prayers or an entire prayer strategy. The Lord might lead you to give a specific gift or offering to a person or ministry, including your home church.

Will you respond? The more you respond to God's leading, the more of His glory you will see. There will be times when He will test us to see if it's "graduation" or "promotion" time in our spiritual life. God wants to take us *"from glory to glory"* (2 Corinthians 3:18), and we must pass His tests to move up!

LAY HOLD OF THE MIRACULOUS

Everything in the kingdom of God is based on how we respond to God and His Word. I am reminded of the New Testament account of the woman with the issue of blood, who said, *"If I may touch but [Jesus's] clothes, I shall be whole"* (Mark 5:28). The moment she touched Jesus, power was released, and she was healed. In another instance, when Jesus was in Gennesaret, the people there *"besought Him that [the sick] might only touch the hem of His garment: and as many as touched were made perfectly whole"* (Matthew 14:36). We must make a decision to press beyond the crowd and the chaos of our days and lay hold of the miraculous.

Like the woman with the issue of blood and the sick in Gennesaret, Jesus desires for us to experience His power. But unlike them, we don't have to wait for an external manifestation to receive our miracle. We have Jesus living inside of us! We must lay hold of the Christ (the Anointed One and His anointing) from within. Releasing God's dunamis power is not a matter of human effort, but a matter of faith and expectancy. The woman with the issue of blood is a spiritual prototype for the supernatural church today and an example of faith in the power of God. Every time we take a step of faith based on the revealed Word of God, we activate God's power in our lives. Without action, power remains merely potential.

EQUIPPED VERSUS ACTIVATED

When I consider the reality of walking in miracles daily, I often think about the difference between being equipped and being activated. Let me explain! Many believers are equipped, but they are not activated. To *equip* means "to supply with the necessary items for a particular purpose" or "to prepare (someone) mentally for a particular situation or task." However, to *activate* means "to make (something) active or operative." Let me share something from my personal life that will help illustrate the difference.

I really enjoy technology! Particularly, I enjoy smartphones and mobile devices. One day, I went to the store to get a new smartphone because my old phone was no longer functioning properly. The sales associate quickly began educating me on all the wonderful features of my new device. His main focus was on how powerful this version of the phone was and the enormous speed of its processor. During the exchange process, they deactivated my old phone so that the information could be transferred over to the new phone. At that point, I remembered that I needed to call my wife and ask her an important question, so I attempted to call her on the new phone. The sales clerk told me, "This phone is not yet activated. Therefore, you cannot use it to make calls right now! You have to wait until the activation is complete." Here was this beautiful phone, with all of its awesome technology, but I was not able to use it!

God used this simple example to teach me a profound truth about the supernatural. Many believers have all the right "equipment"—they have the Word of God and the Holy Spirit—but they have not been activated. In other words, they are not actively operating in the supernatural purpose of God for their lives. Until they are activated, they cannot operate in His miraculous power.

Unfortunately, much of the modern church culture encourages Christians to be stagnant. Some churches have even deactivated believers who were on fire for God. By the time the religious institutions indoctrinated them with defeatist theology, they lost their passion and zeal. Thousands of believers are sitting on their gifts, callings, and anointings while they wait for God to move in their lives.

SECRET TO THE SUPERNATURAL:

THERE ARE CERTAIN MIRACLES YOU WILL NEVER SEE

UNTIL YOU STEP FURTHER INTO THE DEEP.

We have learned that action activates miracles, but we have to do more than just taking random steps in an aimless direction. We must learn to move purposefully according to the Word of God. That is when something supernatural will happen!

Before Peter walked on water, he was equipped. According to Mark 6 and elsewhere, it seems that Jesus had already given Peter and the other disciples spiritual authority prior to that event. However, it wasn't until Peter asked Jesus if he could come to Him on the water, and Peter stepped out in faith, that he saw the law of gravity totally defied. The more we step out, the more God "shows out"! Just as my phone had to receive the full download of software before it could be utilized, you and I must "download" God's Word into our heart if we want to walk in the faith to perform miracles. I am not just talking about seeing sporadic occurrences of miracles, but consistently seeing miracles daily.

REMEMBER: PRAYER RELEASES MIRACLE POWER

We can never understate the power of prayer for daily walking in miracles. In fact, almost every miracle in the Bible was connected to a man or woman who prayed. Our culture has deeply underestimated prayer. Many people see it as a last resort to a crisis situation. Others see it as some superficial religious practice. We must remember that prayer is a secret power of the supernatural—and it is one of the ways in which we become activated in the miraculous.

It was through prayer that my wife and I began to experience miracles in our lives personally and through our ministry. Every Thursday night, we would meet for prayer in our living room and invite other people to come. And God would move in miraculous ways! One person who was barely able to walk was healed supernaturally. Scores of others were healed and delivered as well. Pretty soon, people from all over our city began to gather in our living room on Thursday evenings to enter into God's presence. Eventually, we needed to move to a larger room at a hotel, "and the rest is history" as our church was born.

Everything good that I have in my life today, I attribute to prayer. In addition to praying in our own language, it is very important that we make a consistent habit of praying in tongues. Praying in the Spirit is one of the fastest ways to activate our spirit being. My wife and I began praying in tongues for at least thirty minutes a day, and all sorts of miracles began to happen in our family, finances, church, and ministry. People got healed! People were delivered! The church began to grow. If you don't know where to start when it comes to praying in tongues, I would encourage you to visit SidRoth.org, where you'll find some wonderful teachings and resources on this topic.

Remember that God paid a tremendous price for us to have intimate fellowship with Him and walk in His miraculous power daily! No matter where you are in life or ministry, know that a lifestyle of miracles is possible. God has equipped you through the Holy Spirit, and He desires to activate you today to operate in a dimension that is beyond limitations. Miracles, signs, and wonders will become the norm in your life from this day forward!

PRAYER FOR ACTIVATION

Father, in the name of Jesus, I thank You for who You are and all that You have done in my life. Today is a beautiful day. Today is a new opportunity to walk in Your presence and power. Everything that I need is found in You! By faith, I release Your power in and through my life. I activate the spiritual keys in Your Word that release the miraculous. I submit to the power of Your Word, obey Your precepts, stand on Your promises, and respond to Your divine instructions. I declare that I have been equipped to walk in the supernatural and experience all that You have purposed and predestined for my life. Nothing will separate me from the love of God in Christ Jesus! Every promise in Your Word is "yes and amen." Thank You for activating me in the supernatural, causing me to boldly operate in the culture of the miraculous. Miracles are commonplace through the power of Your presence. Thank You, Father, for moving in my life. In the name of Jesus, amen!

MIRACLE INSIGHTS

1. What are the five keys to activating God's power, and why are they important?

2. Share an example of submission to God from the Bible.

3. What can the woman with the issue of blood teach us about miracles?

4. What is the difference between being equipped and being activated?

SCHOOL OF THE MIRACULOUS PRACTICUM

1. Consider the five keys to activating God's power: (1) submit, (2) obey, (3) expect, (4) stand, and (5) respond. Which of these keys are you in most need of working on? Decide today how you will specifically put this key into practice, and then follow through with it. Periodically review each of these keys to see if you are practicing them.

2. As you think about what you have learned in this book, list the ways in which God has equipped you to walk in the miraculous. Now list the areas in which you have actually been activated to move in the Spirit to see miracles daily. Which areas do you still need to initiate by believing God's Word and stepping out in faith? Move forward in activation so that you can daily walk in miracles!

3. Prayer is a secret power of the supernatural, and one of the ways in which we become activated in the miraculous. What priority do you currently place on prayer? Make a plan to pray regularly. Join with other believers at your church for prayer meetings. If there aren't any prayer meetings at your church, start one yourself with friends, family members, or other church members. Pray for each other's needs and the needs of your community. Ask God to demonstrate His power through your unified prayers that His kingdom would come and His will be done on earth as it is in heaven!

ABOUT THE AUTHOR

Dr. Kynan T. Bridges is the senior pastor of Grace & Peace Global Fellowship in Tampa, Florida. With a profound revelation of the Word of God and a dynamic teaching ministry, Dr. Bridges has revolutionized the lives of many in the body of Christ. Through his practical approach to applying the deep truths of the Word of God, he reveals the authority and identity of the new covenant believer.

God has placed on Dr. Bridges a particular anointing for understanding and teaching the Scriptures, along with the gifts of prophecy and healing. Dr. Bridges and his wife, Gloria, through an apostolic anointing, are committed to equipping the body of Christ to live in the supernatural every day and to fulfill the Great Commission. It is the desire of Dr. Bridges to see the nations transformed by the unconditional love of God.

A highly sought speaker and published author of a number of books, his previous books with Whitaker House include *Invading the Heavens*, *Unmasking the Accuser*, *The Power of Prophetic Prayer*, and *Kingdom Authority*. Dr. Bridges is a committed husband, a mentor, and a father of five beautiful children: Ella, Naomi, Isaac, Israel, and Anna.

Welcome to Our House!

We Have a Special Gift for You

It is our privilege and pleasure to share in your love of Christian books. We are committed to bringing you authors and books that feed, challenge, and enrich your faith.

To show our appreciation, we invite you to sign up to receive a specially selected **Reader Appreciation Gift**, with our compliments. Just go to the Web address at the bottom of this page.

God bless you as you seek a deeper walk with Him!

WE HAVE A GIFT FOR YOU. VISIT:

whpub.me/nonfictionthx

WHITAKER
HOUSE